Despite its small size, this book provides deep and rich reflection on tough texts in the Old Testament. Tackling all the hottest topics head on, Belcher shows that it is atheists, not Christians, who have the toughest case to answer.

Peter J. Williams
Principal, Tyndale House, Cambridge, UK;
author, *Can We Trust the Gospels*

Although the New Atheism has now fizzled out, many of its arguments have spread widely into the culture – not least the idea that the God of the Old Testament is mean, vicious and hateful. In this thorough, well researched book, Richard Belcher explores why this argument fails. It will be a helpful addition to any pastor's library!

Andy Bannister
Director, Solas Centre for Public Christianity, UK

THE BIG TEN
Critical Questions Answered

SERIES EDITORS
James N. Anderson and Greg Welty

Why Does the God of the Old Testament seem so Violent and Hateful?

Richard P. Belcher, Jr.

CHRISTIAN
FOCUS

Copyright © Richard P. Belcher, Jr. 2023

Paperback ISBN 978-1-5270-1016-8
E-book ISBN 978-1-5271-1058-8

10 9 8 7 6 5 4 3 2 1

Published in 2023
by
Christian Focus Publications Ltd,
Geanies House, Fearn, Ross-shire,
IV20 1TW, Great Britain.

www.christianfocus.com

Cover design by Daniel Van Straaten

Printed by Bell and Bain, Glasgow

CONTENTS

Dedication

Dedicated to my family
who lived out in the face of death
the firm belief in the sovereignty of God.

Dedicated to my church family,
Christ Ridge PCA,
who faithfully over the years have been
committed to the power of prayer and the
efficacy of the preached Word of God.

Acknowledgements

There are several people I would like to thank without whose help this book would not have been possible.

I would like to thank Christian Focus, especially Willie MacKenzie, who gave a rookie professor the opportunity to publish and has been a joy to work with over the years.

I would like to thank Dr. James Anderson and Dr. Greg Welty, the two editors of the Big Ten apologetic series, who made invaluable suggestions that greatly improved the final product of this book. Of course, I take full responsibility for its contents.

I would like to thank Will Keyton and Isaac Noh, two Teaching Assistants who have tracked down articles and other sources for this project. Thanks also to Whitney Pegram, Reference Services Specialist for the

RTS Charlotte library, for her timely work in getting resources.

This book is dedicated to two of my closest 'families' whose lives were intertwined in the fall of 2021 when my son-in-law, Michael Dixon, pastor of Christ Ridge PCA in Fort Mill, SC almost died with complications from Covid. My biological family (Belchers, Dixons, and Sewells) lived out what we profess to believe that whatever God ordains is right and that we must trust in His goodness even in the face of losing a husband, father, pastor, and a beloved Christian brother. My church family, Christ Ridge PCA, has over the years shown a commitment to the power of prayer and to confidence in the preached Word of God through which He accomplishes His purposes for His people. In God's great mercy, Michael did not die, and is faithfully back at work as the senior pastor of Christ Ridge Church. To God be all the glory!

Introduction:
The Focus of this Book

Atheism is nothing new. The fact that there are atheists in the world is not surprising, but what is different today, as compared with thirty years ago, is that they are very loud, adamant, and angry. They have no trouble getting into people's faces to denigrate belief in God, to support their atheistic views, and to try to limit the influence of religion in modern society. Globalization and secularization, along with social media that allows people to share their views with a worldwide audience, are some of the factors that have promoted their rise to prominence. Several atheists have been at the forefront of the attack on religion and belief in God. The 'four horsemen' spearheading this movement are Richard Dawkins, Sam Harris, Christopher Hitchens, and Daniel Dennett.[1] They

1. Christopher Hitchens, Richard Dawkins, Sam Harris, and Daniel Dennett, *The Four Horsemen: A Conversation that Sparked an Atheist Revolution* (Random House, 2019).

express themselves with great passion, even anger, and are not afraid to call religion dangerous for human society and something that must be destroyed.[2]

Although they make a lot of noise, the new atheists are not necessarily succeeding in their attempts of eradicating the influence of religion from society. The Western world has seen a progression in secularization, but other parts of the world have seen the growth of Christianity, as well as other religions. Statistics show that China could be a majority-Christian country by 2050. It is projected that by 2060, Christianity will still be the largest belief system with about 32 percent of the world's population. Other religions, like Islam, are also growing. The proportion of humanity identifying as atheists is projected to decline from 16 to 13 percent. Although many Americans are becoming nonreligious, 40 percent of Americans raised nonreligious become religious (typically Christian) as adults, while only 20 percent of those raised Protestant make the switch to atheism. These statistics have led many to argue that secularization has failed to capture the hearts and minds of most people.[3] Whether or not that is true, the new atheists need to be answered.

---

2. Paul Copan, *Is God a Moral Monster? Making Sense of the Old Testament God* (Grand Rapids: Baker Books, 2011), p. 15.

3. For the sources of the statistical evidence see Rebecca McLaughlin, *Confronting Christianity: 12 Hard Questions for the World's Largest Religion* (Wheaton: Crossway, 2019), pp. 11-15.

This book will address some of the specific charges that Dawkins has made against the God of the Bible in his book *The God Delusion*.[4] He is an influential, popular author who is not afraid to state his views with passion, boldness, and bluntness.[5] It is easy to take verses from the Bible out of context, put them on a meme, and make the God of the Bible look like a tyrannical despot. To present an accurate picture of God, we will have to look at how the Bible presents God. The Bible claims to be the revelation of His character and His plan for human beings and the world we live in. Thus, we must honestly examine the Bible's view of God to accurately understand Him. Even if you do not believe what the Bible says, at least you should be concerned with an accurate view of what the Bible says about God; otherwise, you will not be taken seriously by most Christians.

Once we see this fundamental, pervasive, biblical teaching about the character and plan of God, we can also see why Dawkins's charges against God based on certain Old Testament passages lack plausibility. Dawkins displays little awareness of the overall biblical narrative that informs and illuminates the texts he cites. One

---

4. Richard Dawkins, *The God Delusion* (New York: Houghton Mifflin, 2008).

5. Richard Dawkins is included in the Great Thinkers series published by P&R not because he is a great thinker but because of his influence. See Ranson Poythress, *Richard Dawkins* (Phillipsburg: P&R Publishing, 2018), pp. xvii–xix.

main aim of this book is to make this connection clear. By the time you finish chapters 1–3, you will be in a good position to see why Dawkins' charges against God, surveyed in chapters 4 to 6, are implausible.

We will begin in Chapter 1 with a discussion of the goodness of God and its implications for our lives. Chapter 2 will show that God has both the power and the desire to save us from what has held us back from being fulfilled in life. Chapter 3 shows that God's justice is a necessary and beneficial attribute for us to celebrate because it means that the injustices that we face in life will not ultimately triumph. Chapter 4 covers 'texts of violence' on which the charge is made that God is a violent God of genocide, delighting in the destruction of people. Chapter 5 addresses the charge that God is a cruel, racist, and misogynist God who oppresses certain groups of people. Chapter 6 examines the exclusive claims of God and seeks to answer the charge that He is a megalomaniac. Chapter 7 examines the charge that religion is the greatest threat that society faces and shows that getting rid of religion is not the answer to the problems of the world. In fact, horrible relationships develop among people in societies that live without God. We hope to show that the God of the Bible, particularly the God of the Old Testament, is not the moral monster that many have portrayed Him to be. It is impossible to do this without examining the Bible.

I encourage everyone to read the Bible. But be careful, it is a powerful book that has changed people's lives.[6]

---

6. For a riveting example of how the Bible has changed someone's life see Rosaria Butterfield, *The Secret Thoughts of an Unlikely Convert: An English Professor's Journey into Christian Faith*, 2nd ed. (Pittsburgh: Crown & Covenant Publications, 2014); for other examples see William Edgar, *Does Christianity Really Work?* (Ross-shire: Christian Focus Publications, 2016).

1

The Goodness of God: A God Who Provides the Best

The world we live in is a hot mess. I don't know how you respond to that statement, but it is hard to deny. Although sometimes we are insulated from the trouble in the world, the evidence is clear and undeniable. Almost every area of life is affected. Just look at the way people treat each other. Governments try to control what people believe and even put people in prison for not following the official teaching. People are driven by anger, jealousy, and malice leading to assaults, robberies, and murders. Even where you would expect love and kindness, such as the relationship between parents and children, too many cases of abuse occur. Human life is too easily snuffed out by violence. But it is not just human life that is a mess; the world we live in gives evidence that something is wrong. We have witnessed the destructive power of earthquakes, tsunamis, tornadoes, and hurricanes. The spread of new diseases and viruses take many lives every year, and as I wrote this the world had almost come to a standstill because of the coronavirus pandemic. People have lost loved ones, but many are also on the brink of economic collapse. We have come face to face with our helplessness against the forces of nature and the mortality of human life that can so easily succumb to the events of a world over which we have no control. Sometimes it takes cataclysmic events for people to ask, 'What in the world is going on?' Or more specifically, 'What kind of world do I really live in?' Is it a good world, a damaged world, a world out of control? How do we explain the events of the world in which we live? What is wrong with the world?

These questions have been answered in different ways. Some think that the current state of the world is the way the world has always been. Although human beings have been able to improve life in very significant ways, we have not been able to control cataclysmic events like hurricanes or the spread of deadly disease. And no one has a cure for death so that there is little hope for a future that is free from disease or death. Others argue that God, or a belief in God, is the problem. Religion is seen as dangerous to society because the God of the Old Testament is understood as a despicable character who is petty, bloodthirsty, and a malevolent bully.[1] Another view presents a different picture of God and argues that hope for the world exists because of the righteous actions of God who created a world that was not originally subject to tragic events, disease, or even death itself. This view argues that the good world God created has become a damaged world, but it is never out of His control. This chapter hopes to explain this view of the world.

The Bible assumes the existence of God and that He created this vast universe in which we live. The very first verse of the first chapter of the first book of the Bible states, 'In the beginning, God created the heavens and the earth' (Gen. 1:1).[2] The assumption of God's existence does not mean that there is no evidence for His existence. The heavens and earth display the evidence of His power and majesty in the beauty and wonder of creation (Rom. 1:18-20). Human beings understand innately that this God who has created them has moral requirements (Rom. 2:14-16). It is important to understand the type of world God created because this will give us a better understanding of the character of God.

---

1. Richard Dawkins, *The God Delusion* (New York: Houghton Mifflin, 2008).

2. Bible references such as Genesis 1:1 refer to the book called Genesis, to the first chapter of that Bible book, and specifically to the first verse of that chapter. Thus 'bookname xx:yy' refers to chapter xx, verse yy of the book by that name. Most versions of the Bible have a table of contents with page numbers to help readers locate each book by name.

THE GOODNESS OF GOD'S CREATION

Genesis 1 describes the creation of the world that we live in and one word characterizes God's creation – the word 'good'. This word occurs six times in Genesis 1:1-2:3. Light is created on the first day and it is called good (1:4). The dry land and the seas are created on the third day, and they are called good (1:10). The sun, moon, and stars are created on the fourth day, and they are called good (1:18). The great sea creatures and birds are created on the fifth day, and they are called good (1:21). Beasts, livestock, and land animals are created on the sixth day, and they are called good (1:25). After the creation of human beings in the image of God on the sixth day, there is a summary statement that 'God saw everything that he had made and behold, it was very good' (1:31). The pervasive use of this word on almost every day of creation shows that the basic elements of the world at the time of creation are good. The physical universe we live in and the physical bodies we inhabit are 'good'. The word 'good' can be understood in a variety of ways. It can refer to something that is beautiful. Certainly, there are many beautiful things we see in the world in which we live. Sunrises and sunsets are majestic to behold. The ocean itself is both wondrous and beautiful. A great sea creature, like a whale, causes us to marvel at its size, power, and beauty.

The basic elements that make up the world we inhabit are breathtakingly beautiful.

The word 'good' can also mean functional, or beneficial according to something's purpose. The sun rising and setting is not only pleasant to the eyes, but it is also beneficial to the earth. The sun produces heat so that the earth is not a ball of ice. The sun also produces light which helps the human body to produce Vitamin D (necessary for calcium absorption) and it aids the process by which plants synthesize foods from carbon dioxide and water (photosynthesis). This process not only produces oxygen, which is essential for human beings and animals, but many animals also eat the plants for food. The sun is beneficial (good) because it carries out the purpose for which it was created. We could go through all the different things created in Genesis 1 to show their benefit, but not only are individual things called 'good', but everything is called 'good' (Gen. 1:31). In other words, not just the individual parts but also the world itself as a whole is viewed as fulfilling its beneficial purpose. Everything is functioning according to its design. The world is harmonious with each part contributing to the benefit of the whole. In fact, the earth's relationship to the sun is just the right distance to allow life on earth to blossom. If the sun was too close to the earth, we would die of heat, but if the sun was too far away from the earth, we would die from being too cold. Nothing could survive either scenario.[3]

Genesis 1 also highlights the creation of human beings by setting apart their creation from the other things that are created. In other words, when God created the living creatures, He said, 'Let the earth bring forth living creatures … and beasts of the earth … and God made the beasts of the earth' (1:24-25). But when God created human beings, He deliberated with Himself saying, 'Let us make' before He created. Also, human beings are the only ones created in God's image and are given the role of being stewards of God's creation (Gen. 1:26-27). This means that human beings are placed over God's creation to govern it and help bring out the benefits of creation for humanity. The role of human beings is further developed in Genesis 2 where God made a special garden for Adam and gave him the job of caring for the garden by cultivating the plants and the trees that would grow there (Gen. 2:5-9, 15). The garden was also a good place. It was certainly a beautiful place as it grew 'every tree that [was] pleasant to the sight and good for food' (Gen. 2:9). The phrase 'pleasant to the sight' does not use the word 'good' but the phrase means the trees

---

3. For a brief, clear discussion of the fine-tuning of the universe see Ransom Poythress, *Has Science Made God Unnecessary?* (Ross-shire: Christian Focus Publications, 2022), pp. 139-145.

were desirable in appearance; hence, they were beautiful to look at. The word 'good' refers to the benefit of the fruit of the trees for human beings because they provided food. I cannot imagine that they would not also taste good. God wonderfully provided food that would bring nourishment but was also good in appearance and good to the taste. The area in which the Garden of Eden was placed also had gold that was good. Here 'good' takes on all the positive characteristics of being beautiful to look at but also being very beneficial in its use.

The picture presented so far is that God has provided a wonderful world and a beautiful garden for human beings. However, one thing in Genesis 1 and 2 is not good: 'It is not good that the man should be alone' (Gen. 2:18). What is going on here? Genesis 1:1-2:3 gives the bird's eye view of God's creation of the heavens and the earth, including the creation of human beings made in His image and made as male and female. Genesis 2 focuses on how the creation of Adam and Eve took place, including the making of the garden for them and their role in the garden. God first created Adam from the dust of the ground and placed him in the garden to tend and keep it (Gen. 2:15). But Adam cannot fulfill the special role God has given him alone. He needs help in working the garden and in fulfilling God's directive to be fruitful, multiply, and fill the earth (Gen. 1:28). So, God made someone who would complement Adam and help him to fulfill his calling from God. Before God formed Eve, He brought the animals into the Garden for Adam to name them. This is part of his rule over the animals, but it also demonstrates that no helper among the animals was found for him. God must provide his companion, so He fashions Eve from Adam's rib and brings her to him (Gen. 2:19-22). Adam's reaction (Gen. 2:23) shows that God provided just the right complement to him ('bone of my bones, flesh of my flesh'). The fact that it was not good for Adam to be alone is solved. The goodness of God is seen in how He provided everything that Adam and Eve needed to be successful and to flourish.

THE CORRUPTION OF GOD'S GOOD CREATION

The description of the world and the life of Adam and Eve in Genesis 1 and 2 does not match the world in which we live. Although we do experience the beauty of creation and the benefit of family, the life we live is not always harmonious. In fact, life often seems difficult and like an uphill battle. Many times, things work against us as we try to provide for ourselves and our families. Relationships can be stressful. This accurate description of life is explained in Genesis 3, but to explain Genesis 3 we have to go back to Genesis 2. God provided an abundance of trees from which Adam and Eve could eat, but there was one tree from which He commands them not to eat, the tree of knowledge of good and evil (2:9, 17). God was testing them to see if they would honor Him in appreciation for all the good things He had provided for them. He held nothing back from them except this one tree. The name of this tree uses the word 'good' in conjunction with the word 'evil'. The word 'good' here means moral goodness. Here we learn that there is a distinction between good and evil, but we have not yet seen any evidence of it in the world God has created. Will this command of God be obeyed? If not, God declares that death will follow (2:17). The implication is that if they trust God by honoring Him and obeying His command, they will experience even further blessings from God represented in the tree of life. What a momentous decision Adam and Eve face.

Genesis 3 recounts what happens. It introduces a figure called 'the serpent' who is described as 'more crafty than any other beast of the field that the LORD God had made' (3:1). The word 'crafty' has the positive meaning of 'prudent' in Proverbs 12:16, 23 and 14:8, 15, but in Genesis 3 it has a negative meaning. This serpent is different from the other animals not only because he is crafty, but also because he speaks. This raises the question whether the serpent is being used by someone else as an instrument to accomplish his purposes. Later Scriptures will show that behind the serpent is Satan himself, an adversary of God's plans (John 8:43-45; Rev. 12:9).

The serpent approaches Eve to sow doubts in her mind concerning the goodness of God and whether He has her best interests in mind: 'Did God actually say, "You shall not eat of any tree in the garden"?' (3:1). This question emphasizes God's negative command and overlooks the abundant provision of trees that God had given to Adam and Eve for food. Eve corrects the serpent by saying that there is only one tree they cannot eat from (3:2), but she also embellishes God's original command by adding 'neither shall you touch it' (compare 2:17 with 3:3). Perhaps suspicion is growing in her mind because she presents God's command as stricter than it was. The big lie of the serpent comes in an emphatic statement in verse 4: 'You will not surely die'. The serpent's explanation in verse 5 is that God is withholding from Eve the ability to become 'like God, knowing good and evil'. The word 'good' is used here in a moral sense and the word 'know' can mean 'to discern' (Isa. 7:15). Eve begins to believe that she can become like God with the ability to discern for herself what is good and evil. In other words, she does not have to submit to what God has determined as good and evil. The lure of this offer is compounded by the fact that the forbidden tree was very desirable: good for food, a delight to the eyes, and able to make one wise (3:6). This tree was beautiful to look at and seemed to be beneficial for food and wisdom. Eve correctly describes the world as God created it, but she rejects God's right to determine how she should use it.

Eve believed the lie of the serpent, ate from the tree, and gave some to her husband to eat. In her rebellion against God, she rejected God's functional, beneficial purpose of the tree. Disobedience to God's command had immediate negative consequences. Something changed within them, 'Then the eyes of both were opened, and they knew that they were naked.' Because of their disobedience they experienced guilt and shame. Guilt is both a condition that results from breaking God's law and it is a feeling of being ashamed for doing wrong. They knew something was wrong, so they tried to cover their nakedness by sewing fig leaves together (3:7). Their relationship to God changed. The next time He came into the Garden they hid themselves from His presence (3:8). Their relationship with each other changed. Adam blamed Eve for what had happened, and Eve blamed the serpent (3:12-13). They did not take responsibility for their actions. Their ability to carry out the mandate God had given them becomes difficult because creation itself is affected by their disobedience. Work is now hard because the ground is cursed and bearing children is full of travail and pain. God's good gift of marriage is now a battlefield of conflicting desires (3:16-19). They also face a hostile spiritual enemy who will try to destroy them (3:15). All of this describes the spiritual death they experienced when they disobeyed God, and they also face the coming prospect of physical death whereby they will return to the dust of the ground (3:19). Their disobedience to God brings devastating consequences.

These consequences are also exhibited in their children and descendants. In Genesis 4, Cain murdered his brother Abel because he became angry that God accepted Abel's offering and not his offering. Through the line of Cain, the negative consequences of being disobedient to God escalates. Cain and his family are driven away from the presence of God. One of his descendants, Lamech, takes more than one wife (against Gen. 2:24) and boasts of killing a young man for wounding him (4:23-24). By Genesis 6, the wickedness of human beings is described as great on the earth and every intention of the thoughts of human hearts was only evil continually (6:5). Disobedience to God spread far and wide and affected everything and everyone.

IMPLICATIONS FOR OUR LIVES

It is helpful at this point to stop and draw some conclusions from the first several chapters of Genesis.[4] The world

---

4. Some readers may be skeptical about the historicity of Adam and Eve; if so, see Richard Phillips, ed., *God, Adam, and You: Biblical*

that God created was good. It was wondrously beautiful and everything in the world harmoniously functioned according to its created design. God provided a special garden for Adam and Eve and provided everything they needed to live together in the garden and to fulfill the work that He gave them to do. They had an opportunity to show their gratitude to God by obeying the command that He had given to them. He had provided an abundance of food in numerous fruit trees but withheld one tree from them to test their loyalty. Their disobedience to God changed everything and the results explain the condition of our world today. The violence we see among human beings every day was not the way God originally made us. The disruptions of nature in hurricanes, earthquakes, and tsunamis are not the way the world was originally made. The hardship of human life in exhausting labor, difficulty in childbirth, and sickness and disease come because of rebellion against God. The angst, anxiety, and fear that humans experience are a result of living in a world that is estranged from God. It is important to understand that the world as we experience it today is not the way God created it but is a result of human ingratitude toward the goodness of God. If Adam and Eve had followed God they

---

Creation Defended and Applied (Phillipsburg: P&R Publishing, 2015) and Terry Mortenson, ed., *Searching for Adam: Genesis and the Truth about Man's Origin* (Green Forest: Master Books, 2016).

would have experienced even more of God's blessings, would have secured the abundant life God had provided for them, and would have been able to eat from the tree of life. The miserable condition of the world in which we live is a result of the desire for humans to live the way they want to live apart from God.

Perhaps you are thinking: Why would one act of disobedience plunge the world into chaos? Why is my life affected so much by Adam's decision? Is that fair? Those are good questions. First, it is clear in Genesis 1 to 3 that Adam acts as a representative for Eve and for his descendants. The personal name 'Adam' is also used in a generic sense to refer to 'mankind' or human beings as male and female: 'so God created mankind (*'ā<u>d</u>ām*) in his own image ... male and female he created them' (Gen. 1:27).[5] Adam was formed first and the command not to eat from the tree of knowledge of good and evil was given to him before Eve was created (Gen. 2:15-17). This does not mean that Eve was inferior to Adam, but that Adam was designated by God as the representative. Even though Eve was deceived and sinned first by eating of the fruit, God addressed Adam when He confronted them with their disobedience (Gen. 3:9). Ultimately, the buck stops with Adam. The fact that someone can act

---

5.   This is my translation of Genesis 1:27. If not specified, I will use the English Standard Version translation of the Bible.

as a representative for someone else is common today. When the president of a country declares war on another country, all the citizens of that country are technically at war with the other country because the president acts as their representative. A representative is authorized to speak and act for someone else. When my mother came down with Alzheimer's my wife was appointed by our local state government as her legal guardian. She acted on behalf of my mother in every area of her life, including her living arrangements, health, and finances. This kind of a relationship is similar to what the Bible calls a covenant, and it operates on the basis of representation.[6] So, Adam was our representative acting on our behalf.

The next question is why would one act of disobedience lead to such devastating results for not just Adam and Eve, but for all of creation? It is hard for us to understand the reprehensible act of rebellion against the goodness and authority of God in Genesis 3. By his disobedience, Adam rejected the God who had provided everything for him. Instead, he wanted to decide for himself what was right and wrong. In other words, he wanted to live his life apart from God. He wanted to be the master of his own fate. Just imagine a bride and groom on their wedding day making

---

6. For more on this, see: Richard P. Belcher, Jr., *The Fulfillment of the Promises of God: An Explanation of Covenant Theology* (Ross-shire: Christian Focus Publications, 2020), pp. 33-5.

vows to love and support each other for the rest of their lives, enjoying the festivities of the wedding ceremony, but that night the groom goes out on the town to find someone else to spend the night with, leaving the bride alone in her room. What an insult! It shows that the groom is not satisfied with his bride. Instead of adoring her and loving her, he treats her rudely and shows what he really thinks about her. Adam's act of rebellion was a traitorous act that showed a lack of appreciation for all that God had provided for him.

If we were snubbed the way the bride was or treated as insignificant the way that Adam treated God, we would probably wash our hands of the whole mess and say we are done with it. God could have reacted that way. He could have abandoned His creation and left Adam and Eve to experience the full force of their rebellion, but instead He reacted with grace. Grace is many times defined as 'unmerited favor', which is to treat someone with favor who does not deserve it. But further, grace can be defined as 'demerited favor', which is favor shown to someone who has acted in a faithless, traitorous way where it is clear they deserve condemnation and death. Although Adam and Eve experienced the consequences of their sin, God did not destroy them immediately, but allowed them to continue to live. When they tried to cover up the effects of their sin and guilt with fig leaves, God provided animal skins (3:21) to foreshadow the way of true redemption (the act of delivering from sin) through the shedding of blood (Heb. 9:22). God also promised that someone would come to defeat the serpent (3:15). God had a plan that would eventually lead to the full restoration of His relationship to human beings and to creation itself in a new heaven and new earth. The foundation of that plan is laid out in the Old Testament in preparation for the coming Redeemer. The initial fulfillment of that plan takes place in the first coming of Christ who died as a sacrifice for our sin. Christ ends our warfare with God. The consummation of that plan comes in the second coming of Christ when He will establish the new heavens and new earth. All the difficult texts of the Old Testament must be understood considering God's good and gracious plan to restore His relationship to human beings who hate Him and want to go their own way.[7] He establishes covenants and is faithful to the promises He makes as He pursues those who have rejected Him.

Perhaps you have thought that it is not fair that Adam would be your representative. Why do you have to face the consequences of the results of his actions?

---

7. We will see in later chapters that understanding the relevance of God's salvation plan for the particulars of Old Testament history is essential to exposing the weak reasoning of the four atheist 'horsemen' previously mentioned.

It is a good question. Firstly, even though Adam's action affected you in many ways, each of us should recognize that we love to go our own way. We love to set our own agenda and to decide for ourselves what is right and good. God has given to us His law and we have all too easily broken it. In other words, when we go against God's way, we do it willingly. We too are guilty and are held accountable for our own rebellion against God. But secondly, the good news is that we can receive something that we do not deserve. If we believe in Jesus and what He has accomplished for us, that He has fulfilled the law that we have broken, and that He has died on the cross to pay the penalty for our sin and guilt, then we receive His righteousness. God declares the guilty to be not guilty because He does not see our rebellion, but He sees us in Christ. It does not seem fair that we should benefit from what Christ has done, but this is God's plan of salvation. We do not deserve anything that we receive from Christ. The goodness of God that shines in Genesis 1 and 2 continues to be shown to a world that has rejected Him. The problem with the world is not God's fault. We have messed it up, but God has provided the solution to the problems of the world. God's good world has been corrupted by human rebellion and it seems out of control, but God's plan of salvation will be accomplished.

SUMMARY OF MAIN POINTS

- The world God created was good, both in its beauty and in the beneficial functioning of the elements of creation.

- Human beings are unique in God's creation because they are made in His image and are stewards over creation.

- Even though God provided everything that Adam and Eve needed to flourish, they disobeyed God, which brought devastating consequences into their lives and the world.

- God has a gracious plan to restore not only His relationship with human beings but also all of creation so that it will function the way it was originally created to function.

2

The Power and Grace of God: A God Able and Willing to Save

On Wednesday morning, October 14, 1987, Baby Jessica, only eighteen months old, became the most famous child in the United States.[1] Playing in the backyard of her aunt's home with four other children, she fell into a well that was only eight inches in diameter and became trapped twenty-two feet below ground in the shaft of the well. Beneath layers of rock harder than granite, the rescue mission was extraordinarily difficult, and at times it seemed impossible. Only extraordinary measures would be able to save Baby Jessica from that narrow well.

Besides pumping oxygen into the well and trying to maintain contact with Baby Jessica, rescuers drilled a 30-inch wide, 29-foot-deep shaft parallel to the well.

---

1. Most of the information for this story came from https://www. biography.com/personality/baby-jessica.

This took six hours, then the difficult part was trying to drill a horizontal tunnel from the shaft to two feet below the well where she was trapped. This could not be accomplished with jackhammers. It took a mining engineer and the use of a relatively new technology called 'waterjet cutting' to cut the horizontal tunnel. Forty-five hours after falling into the well, the shaft and the tunnel were completed. Medical personnel grew alarmed because dehydration and shock were becoming greater dangers to Baby Jessica than the entrapment itself. When rescuers finally reached her, they could not pull her out because of the way her body was wedged in the shaft. The health technicians checked her vital signs and then gave the order, 'Pull hard! She does not have more time. You may have to break her to save her'.[2] Fifty-eight hours after Jessica fell into the well, she became free.

Baby Jessica faced certain death unless people with the ability, know-how, and equipment could rescue her. With a young life in danger, they were very determined to save her, but, even then, it was a close call. She almost did not survive. We face a much more serious situation, even a situation that is impossible from a human standpoint, because we do not have the ability to deliver ourselves from the power of corruption. As we saw in the last

2. Bryan Chapell, *Christ-Centered Preaching: Redeeming the Expository Sermon*, 3rd ed. (Ada: Baker, 2018), p. 167.

chapter, God created the world good and gave to human beings the ability to live for Him. Human rebellion against God brought into the world all the negative consequences of wickedness that affected every aspect of our lives. We now face living in a broken world amid broken relationships with the looming prospect of death hanging over us. We see the effects of corruption in the world and, if we are honest with ourselves, we see this corruption in our own lives. The power of corruption has made us slaves to the evil intentions of our hearts (Rom. 6:16). We are 'children of wrath' who are spiritually dead (Eph. 2:1-3), without any ability to free ourselves from the power of corruption and the sentence of death. In other words, we are very much like Baby Jessica caught in that shaft and unable to free herself by her own power. As adults we are both helpless and responsible for our lives without the ability to fix our situation. This is the truth we must affirm about human beings in general, but also about ourselves, if we are going to understand the glorious salvation that God has planned.

If corruption is a strong enslaving power we experience in our lives, then we need a God who can deliver us from it. The good news is that God has a plan to save us from our own wickedness and to salvage creation by giving hope for a future free from corruption and death. He instituted that plan in Genesis 3:15 and will bring that plan to completion at the end of history. The question this chapter addresses is whether the God who reveals Himself in Scripture is able and willing to accomplish this plan of salvation. Does God have the ability to carry out His plan of restoration to deliver us and creation from the bondage of corruption? The next chapter will discuss how He will accomplish this great plan of salvation. Understanding the character of God and His desire for creation is important when discussing some of the passages of the Old Testament that cause people to question His character.

A God Able to Save

We want to explore several aspects of God's character in this chapter to show that He is fully capable of carrying out His plan of salvation. The first is His power. We are confronted with His power every day because we live in the world He created. It is humbling to look at the earth from outer space. It looks very small in the vast universe in which it exists. I am always amazed when I fly in a plane how small human activity looks from 10,000 feet. As the plane descends to land, one can see the cars and trucks traveling on the interstates and they look no bigger than ants. The earth itself is full of marvelous but deadly wonders, from the power of a severe thunderstorm to the destruction of a tornado or hurricane. I will never forget the overwhelming sense of awe that came over me when I stood before the Grand Canyon. The immensity of that canyon was unbelievable.

The Bible teaches that God has created the world in which we live (Gen. 1:1) and aspects of His character, particularly His eternal power and divine nature, are clearly revealed in creation (Rom. 1:19-20). This is called 'general revelation'. Even if someone does not believe in God, he or she is confronted with God's power and deity just by living in the world He has created. This part of God's character is plain to people because they clearly perceive these divine characteristics in the things that have been made. It is like an artist whose work of art manifests her ability, style, and characteristics. God's eternal power and divine nature are revealed in the world we live. We see certain things in creation, and we intuitively know that a being who is greater than a mortal human brought this universe into existence. The wonder and awe of creation, from the smallest cell to the enormous galaxy in which we live, confronts us daily with the existence of a God who has left a clear testimony of His power and deity.

'Wait a minute,' you might say, 'I don't recognize these attributes of God in the universe and the people I talk to don't see them either.' The reason for this goes back to our rebellion against God when we became enemies of

God. Because of our opposition to God, we suppress the knowledge of God's power and deity that we receive from God's creation. In other words, the knowledge is clear but we refuse to see it and so we live our lives as if it is not there. Thus, although God's power and deity are clearly seen when one views the Grand Canyon, or looks into outer space, many will hold off that knowledge and provide other explanations for what they see. And yet, at the core of every human being, who is made in God's image, is this 'sense of deity' that continues to confront every one of us.

Although enough knowledge is presented to us from the created world that we are without excuse before God (Rom. 1:20), there is not enough knowledge to tell us about God's glorious plan to rescue us from our slavery to corruption. This knowledge comes from what is called God's 'special revelation,' in the form of the Scriptures of the Old and New Testaments. Without this knowledge we are like an artist in a dark cave trying to paint a picture of something we cannot see. Even a small glimmer of light brings clarity. So, God's revelation in Scripture tells us about His character and the way He plans to redeem His wayward and lost creation. It confirms the knowledge of God's power and deity that we see in creation. Psalm 115:3 states, 'Our God is in the heavens; he does all that he pleases'. 1 Chronicles 29:11 asserts:

> Yours, O LORD, is the greatness and the power
> and the glory and the victory and the majesty,
> for all that is in the heavens and in the earth is
> yours. Yours is the kingdom, O LORD, and you
> are exalted as head above all ... In your hand are
> power and might, and in your hand it is to make
> great and to give strength to all.

God is the exalted king over His creation, and He has the power to accomplish His purpose to deliver those who are in bondage to corruption. He can give victory to those who are broken and defeated. He can give strength to those who are weak and in despair. He is all-powerful and nothing in His universe can hinder His redemption plan. We can have confidence in His ability to accomplish it.

Other aspects of God's character are revealed in the Bible. The amazing thing is that what we learn about the character of God is precisely what is needed for God to carry out His plan of salvation. This makes perfect sense because we who needed to be rescued from the slavery of corruption are made in His image. God created us and so He understands how we are made and what we need to be delivered. The discussion of God's character should not take place in a vacuum. We need to recognize that everything we learn about God helps us better understand our plight and His solution to restore our relationship with Him.

God is a God of truth. He declares that He speaks the truth, 'I the LORD speak the truth; I declare what is right' (Isa. 45:19). The Word that God speaks also takes on the character of truth, 'your word is truth' (John 17:17). It is not surprising that Jesus Christ, the Son of God, can Himself declare, 'I am the way, and the truth, and the life' (John 14:6) and that God would want truth to be a characteristic of His people, 'Speak the truth to one another' (Zech. 8:16). The church is even called 'a pillar and buttress of the truth' (1 Tim. 3:15). This means that God's knowledge of the world and His understanding of our situation in the world is true and accurate. His view is the correct view so that when He speaks concerning the problems we face in the world and the solution to those problems, we need to listen to what He says. Truth is foundational to the discussion that follows because without a recognition of the truth of our corruption, there can be no restoration, no justice, and no liberty.

We also need to understand the holiness of God. The word 'holy' means to be 'set apart' and it describes the uniqueness of God's character. Although we are like God because we are made in His image, He is very different from us or from anything else in creation. God is not part of creation but is transcendent over it. He is high and lifted up (Isa. 6:1) and exalted above the peoples of the world (Ps. 99:1-3). His enthronement on high means He rules over everything. Thus, He is not limited by anything, and He does not need anything. God's unique character can be expressed by several phrases.[3] God is self-existent: He is life and possesses life, and He is the giver of life (John 5:26). As the author of life God has authority over all life. God is self-sufficient: He is complete and self-contained, having within Himself everything He needs (Acts 17:25). God is self-content: He is satisfied within Himself and needs nothing outside of Himself to be content (1 Tim. 6:15-16). He is free from inward frustration and no anxiety weighs Him down. God is self-giving: He delights in His creation and provides everything we need for life (John 1:4), including eternal life beyond life in this world (John 11:25).

God is also holy in His moral perfection. He is unique in that He has no faults, and is completely pure in His thoughts, words, and decisions (Deut. 32:4; Hab. 1:13). He is marked by moral excellency in His being, nature, and motives. His actions are always perfect and His judgments are always right.[4] He expresses the moral perfection of His character in His 'perfect law' (James 1:25). When Isaiah saw God sitting upon His throne, he also heard the angelic creatures that surround His throne cry, 'Holy, holy, holy is the LORD of hosts, the whole earth is full of his glory!' (Isa. 6:3). When John saw

---

3. Steven J. Lawson, *Show Me Your Glory: Understanding the Majestic Splendor of God* (Sanford: Reformation Trust, 2020), pp. 43-52.
4. Ibid., pp. 89-90.

the throne room in heaven, with flashes of lightning and peals of thunder coming from the throne, he also heard the cry, 'Holy, holy, holy is the Lord God Almighty, who was and is and is to come' (Rev. 4:8).

A GOD WILLING TO SAVE

A majestic, transcendent God who is morally perfect would not seem to be a God who is approachable by those who do not meet His standard of perfection. When Isaiah saw the splendor of God's holiness, the contrast with the reality of his own unholy life is expressed in his exclamation:

> Woe is me! For I am lost; for I am a man of unclean lips and I dwell in the midst of a people of unclean lips; for my eyes have seen the King, the LORD of hosts! (Isa. 6:5)

When we understand the holiness of God, we see the failings of our own corruption. We should feel 'lost' or 'undone' because our security in our own goodness is shattered. God rearranges our view of ourselves and the world in which we live. Such an experience may be God's way to reorient our lives toward His salvation. Although we should fear being condemned because of our actions, God has provided a way to take care of our corruption and to bring us into fellowship with Him (see the next chapter). The only way this can happen is because God is a God of grace and steadfast love.

Although we are in a hopeless condition because we are unable to save ourselves, God actively seeks to deliver us. To understand this aspect of God's character, we must understand 'grace' and 'steadfast love' to show how God demonstrates them in His actions. A common definition of grace (*ḥen* in Hebrew and *charis* in Greek) is 'unmerited favor'. This describes favor shown to someone who has not earned it. If you see someone in the parking lot of a grocery store who is about to drop a bag of groceries and you stop to help them, you have acted in a gracious way. You do not know this person, and she has not earned your favor. However, if you are the person who gets paid to help people get groceries to their car, then your actions are not gracious because your favor was earned. You did what you were paid to do. Grace defined as 'unmerited favor' is good, but another element needs to be added. Grace is not just unmerited favor, but it can also be described as 'demerited favor'. This describes favor shown toward someone who is actively opposed to you. You see someone in the parking lot of a grocery store who needs help, you stop to help him, and even though he curses you out, you are still willing to help. The best way to describe God's relationship to us is that He shows favor to those who are actively opposed to Him.

The Bible presents God's relationship with us in the context of our rebellion against Him. God provided everything that Adam and Eve needed in a wonderful place called the Garden of Eden, but they chose to rebel against Him by disobeying His Word. They really believed they could find their own way without God. He could have brought an immediate end to their existence, but He pursued them, forgave them, clothed them, and promised to send someone to defeat the serpent (Gen. 3:15). God showed grace to rebellious sinners. After God had delivered Israel from the power of Egyptian slavery and brought them to the land He had promised them, Israel rejected their mission to take the land because they did not believe in the promises of God. Even though they saw the demonstration of the power of God in the plagues of Egypt, they rejected all the wonderful things God had done for them in the wilderness. God could have destroyed Israel, but He demonstrates faithfulness by using the next generation to fulfill His promises. Israel frequently spurned God's covenant promises and acted as traitors, but God continued to show grace. Paul, who wrote significant portions of the New Testament, affirms the nature of God's grace in Ephesians 2 where he describes all of humanity as being dead in trespasses and sins (2:1). Spiritual death means that in ourselves we have no interest in God, no desire for God, no intent on pleasing God, and no ability to love God. Rather, thinking we are free, we are really under the control of Satan himself who is at work in the sons of disobedience (2:2). We live in the passions of our flesh, carrying out the corrupt desires of our body and mind. Sin so dominates our lives that we are characterized as being by nature children of wrath because we are enemies of God. It is imperative we understand the true condition of corrupt humanity to truly understand God's grace. In addressing the Ephesian believers, Paul describes them as having completely forsaken God before transitioning to God's grace. The transition comes with a marvelous BUT:

> But God, being rich in mercy, because of the great love with which He loved us, even when we were dead in our trespasses, made us alive together with Christ – by grace you have been saved … (Eph. 2:4-5).

God demonstrates His grace to those who hate Him and do not want to have anything to do with Him. This is the consistent response of God throughout all the Bible toward undeserving rebels.

God's gracious character is also exemplified in His abundant and surprising love and generosity toward those who are in great need. This aspect of God's character is demonstrated in the word *ḥesed*, which is translated as 'steadfast love'. Such love is freely given and is in many ways unexpected. When Rahab of Jericho hid the

Israelite spies, deceived the authorities, and assisted their escape, she had no prior obligation to treat them this way (Josh. 2:12-14). She showed abundant, even unexpected generosity toward the spies. In a greater way, God shows abundant, surprising generosity to people who are in great need, even to people who have rejected Him.

Of the many times God demonstrated His steadfast love, two stand out. The golden calf incident occurred right after God had delivered His people from Egyptian slavery, brought them to Mt. Sinai to enter a covenant with them and, in response, they committed themselves to do all that God had said (Exod. 19:5). While Moses was on Mt. Sinai receiving God's law, the people grew impatient and made other gods for themselves to worship. They held a great feast and celebrated their gods who they claimed brought them up from Egypt (Exod. 32:7-8). Their rejection of God was deliberate and inexcusable. God did not have to show them compassion, but He acted in an unexpected way by showing abundant steadfast love. Thus, Exodus 34:6 affirms that the LORD is 'a God merciful and gracious, slow to anger, and abounding in steadfast love and faithfulness'. What a blessing when abundant, unexpected, undeserved grace is shown when justice is deserved. The reason God could show grace when justice was deserved will be discussed later, but here we must recognize that grace and mercy are at the heart of God's character.

Hosea was a prophet to God's people during a time when God's people had rejected God for the false god Baal. The worship of Baal likely included promiscuous sexual activity to spur Baal to grant fertility to the land. Truth became a rare commodity as people's lives reflected the treachery of unfaithfulness. Hosea describes it this way:

> There is no faithfulness or steadfast love, and no knowledge of God in the land; there is swearing, lying, murder, stealing, and committing adultery; they break all bounds and bloodshed follows bloodshed. Therefore, the land mourns and all who dwell in it languish (Hosea 4:2-3).

To illustrate the situation, God tells Hosea to marry a woman whose life reflects the sexual unfaithfulness of the times. Although Hosea is faithful to his wife, named Gomer, she is not faithful to him but runs after other lovers to provide for her needs. She abandons her faithful and loving husband to seek satisfaction and security from many other men (described in Hosea 2 as parallel to Israel's relationship to the LORD). Instead of finding peace and contentment, she is abused by other men. The marriage relationship is supposed to be an exclusive covenant relationship because each spouse makes promises and oaths to each other to be faithful. God's covenant with Israel was also supposed to be an exclusive relationship. Instead of faithfulness, Israel acted like Gomer and pursued other gods. Even though the LORD provided all that Israel needed, she was not satisfied with His provision but sought security in the pursuit of false gods (Hosea 2:5, 8-9). She broke her covenant relationship with the LORD. Both Hosea and the LORD would have been fully justified in divorcing their spouses, the former for physical adultery and the latter for spiritual adultery. Both had been rejected. The surprising response is that God told Hosea to go rescue Gomer from a difficult situation by purchasing her freedom and bringing her back to himself (3:1). God also pursued Israel. Instead of washing His hands of the whole affair, or even punishing her according to the stipulations of the covenant (Deut. 27-28), He sought to allure her back by speaking tenderly to her. He promised her future blessings, including becoming God's people again (Hosea 2:14-23). Such abundant mercy and steadfast love (*hesed* is used in 2:19) is unexpected, and beyond anything that would be required or expected from God. He is the jilted lover who time and time again has been rejected, but He keeps pursuing His people.

Any discussion of the character of God in the Old Testament must include His goodness, His ability to restore wayward human beings (His power and holiness) and His willingness to pursue them (His grace and steadfast love). Baby Jessica's situation was hopeless. Apart from those who had the ability and the willing determination to do whatever was needed to save her, she would have died trapped in that hole. We are trapped in our own corruption and are powerless to free ourselves. We are dependent on a God who is able to save us and who is willing to save us. Unless God does what is necessary to deliver us, we too will die, enslaved to our wicked ways. One other aspect of the character of God needs to be discussed to understand how a righteous God can save corrupt, unworthy sinners. In the next chapter we will consider that aspect of God's character.

SUMMARY OF MAIN POINTS

- God's power is demonstrated in His works of creation which gives us assurance that He can deliver us from our corruption.

- God's revelation in the Bible confirms His power and tells us about His plan to restore us.

- God is a God of truth which means He speaks the truth about our problems and the solution to those problems.

- God is set apart (holy) from us in many of His attributes which means He is not limited by anything nor is He dependent on anything in creation.

- Although we are not able to deliver ourselves from the bondage of corruption, God is willing to deliver us by His grace.

- God's grace is repeatedly shown to people who have rejected Him and are His enemies.

3

The Justice of God:
Necessary for Salvation

Just about everyone has a deep-seated sense of fairness. We especially react when we believe we ourselves are not treated fairly. When my daughters were growing up, I regularly heard one of them say, 'But that's not fair!' We also react to situations where we think someone else is not treated fairly, particularly when those who are in power use their position to abuse someone in a weaker position. Child abuse cases are particularly heart-wrenching. One such horrendous case was when a four-year old girl was tormented, tortured, and terrorized by her mother's boyfriend while she was away training for the Army Reserves. The little girl died from her injuries. One of the deputies responding to the call broke down on the witness stand, testifying that, 'It's the most horrifying thing I've ever seen done to a human being – especially a child'. When the boyfriend was arrested, he mocked the officers saying, "'What are y'all gonna do? Tie me down and cut me up?'"[1] We appropriately respond with outrage when the home, which is supposed to be a safe and secure place for children, becomes a place of terror. But have you ever wondered, 'Where does our sense of fairness come from? Why do we respond with outrage to such horrible acts of injustice?' At the beginning of this chapter, we will focus on the inability of Darwinists to account for justice and morality before we discuss the justice of God. Even though they criticize the justice of God in the Old Testament, they have deep problems of their own in establishing morality and justice.

A NATURALISTIC VIEW OF MORALITY

It is hard to argue for principles of right and wrong from a materialist view of the world where all that exists is matter. Natural selection, which is the driving force of the theory of evolution, is the process whereby organisms adapt to their environment in a way that ensures a greater likelihood of their survival (the survival of the fittest). This process, along with mutations, is supposed to explain the evolutionary development of all life from a

---

1. This story is taken from https://www.wral.com/deputy-tortured-child-s-injuries-most-horrifying-thing-i-ve-ever-seen-/13452150/

common source, moving from simple to more complex organisms, leading to the production of new species, until human beings are produced from lower forms. Richard Dawkins, a strong proponent of Darwinian evolution, argues that natural selection is powerful enough to create all the complexity we see in the world around us. He does not understand natural selection as a chance process, but as the non-random filtering of random variation. It works because improvement is cumulative and gradual over long periods of time.[2]

Adherents of natural selection argue that it made sense for our prehistoric ancestors to be generous and good to their own group. It also made sense to treat groups outside their own group with harshness and cruelty. Such treatment would ensure your group's survival over against other groups. However, Dawkins also argues that altruistic feelings of love, generosity, and compassion developed through the mechanism of natural selection. Genes that predispose individuals to act in certain ways were favored. Treating outsiders with kindness became beneficial because you would then be treated in a similar way (you scratch my back, and I will scratch yours). People could even develop reputations for

---

2. Dawkins expresses these thoughts in *The God Delusion* (New York: Houghton Mifflin Publishing, 2006), pp. 76, 245 and *Brief Candle in the Dark: My Life in Science* (New York: Harper Collins, 2015), p. 417.

altruistic giving that would enhance their standing in the eyes of others. This Darwinian survival value fostered a good reputation, which in true naturalistic fashion is not just confined to humans but can also apply to animals (see below). Such altruistic inclinations are only rules of thumb which work to promote the genes that built them, but they are seen as misfirings. Such misfirings are blessed Darwinian mistakes that continue to influence us today even where circumstances make them inappropriate to their original function. They have been filtered through the civilizing influences of literature, custom, law, and tradition, and can even be called our 'moral sense'.[3]

THE IMPORTANCE OF UNIVERSAL MORAL PRINCIPLES

Although Dawkins argues that natural selection is not a chance process because the goal is survival of the species, it is dependent upon and cannot accomplish anything apart from chance mutations. The 'moral sense' that Dawkins affirms is not morality in the traditional sense where unchanging, universal principles of right and wrong come from a Creator. In fact, an external moral standard is not required, and such standards would not make sense to the way natural selection works in evolution.[4] Even if

---

3.   Dawkins, *The God Delusion*, pp. 250-4.
4.   Mitch Stokes, *How to Be an Atheist: Why Many Skeptics Aren't Skeptical Enough* (Wheaton: Crossway, 2016), p. 174-5.

in our evolutionary development there appears to be a consensus of moral principles, they cannot be universal moral principles that are *required* behavior for everyone. If a society of people decide that murder is wrong, they can enforce it, but there will always be groups that argue that some murder may be good and appropriate, such as murdering Jews, children in the womb, or children who are born with birth defects. If no universal moral principle against murder exists, then the group that has the most power will enforce their view on others. Condemnation of murder may be a misfiring of evolution but that does not make it evil because evolution cannot support universal truth, only adaptation.[5] To stand against someone who is oppressing you takes more than just 'this is my opinion' or 'this is what is best for my group'. There is power in truth. It is the truth that gives people the courage to stand against evil and it is the truth that sets people free.

Without universal moral principles it is difficult to hold people responsible for their actions. Darwinian evolution can only attempt to explain why things are the way they are, not why some things are morally better than others.[6] Just to assert that certain things are wrong, even if God does not

---

5. Ransom Poythress, *Richard Dawkins* (Phillipsburg: P&R Publishing, 2018), pp. 117, 57.

6. Scott Hahn and Benjamin Wiker, *Answering the New Atheism: Dismantling Dawkins' Case Against God* (Steubenville: Emmaus Road Publishing, 2008), p. 120.

59

exist, begs the question: Where does morality come from?[7] If 'morality' is a product of natural selection, then such morality cannot be universal. The likelihood is that any morality will evolve into other principles that will be more advantageous to our species at a future date. It is difficult to argue that the altruistic good that many live their lives by now is the highest morality because there is no external standard by which to judge it as the highest. Whatever is considered morally good will no doubt evolve as our species develops.

Dawkins explains the altruistic behavior of animals in light of its survival value. One example is the reciprocal altruism displayed in the symbiotic relationship between smaller cleaner fish and their larger fish clients. Both benefit from this relationship.[8] Once animals are brought into the equation in discussing 'morality', it becomes more difficult to argue for universal, or even special principles, for humans over against animals. Some Darwinians, such as Peter Singer, want to erase any distinctions between animals and humans but in the long run humans will end up being treated as animals. It seems arbitrary to argue that we should live to reduce suffering in the most effective means possible when animals, such as lions and bears, continue to hunt and kill for their food. The belief that human beings are made in the image of God

---

7. Stokes, *How to Be an Atheist*, p. 162-4.

8. Dawkins, *The God Delusion*, p. 250.

is what sets humans apart from animals and gives us our dignity. We understand our role in the world as His image bearers according to His gracious purpose that we live a fulfilled life according to His design. Apart from a correct understanding of God's goodness, power, and grace we will not understand how God's design for human beings relates to the more difficult passages in the Old Testament that express His justice. In addition, nothing will keep us from treating each other as less than human because without God human beings act as if they are God.[9]

MORAL PRINCIPLES OR A MATTER OF PREFERENCE?

The point of this discussion is not that atheists cannot live in a way that exhibits love, generosity, and compassion. Atheists can be kind and caring, but do they have justification for living that way based on their atheistic assumptions?[10] If morals do not have to be absolute, as Dawkins argues,[11] then what is right today is due to current social, cultural, and historical consensus. Such

---

9. Poythress, *Richard Dawkins*, p. 18.

10. Atheists might respond that Christians have an internal problem with their worldview because the God they worship behaves immorally by their own Christian standards. The chapters that follow will address this concern considering the character of God laid out in chapters 1-3. For an answer to the problem that Christians do not always act according to the standards set out in the Bible, see Mark Coppenger, *If Christianity Is So Good, Why Are Christians So Bad?* (Ross-shire: Christian Focus Publications, 2022).

11. Dawkins, *The God Delusion*, p. 265.

consensus changes easily as we have seen in the last fifty years where things that were once rejected are now accepted and celebrated. And if you do not go along with these changes, you can easily be 'cancelled', even losing your job if you happen to say something against the politically correct views of the day. A few atheists have begun to recognize that they have been living a 'noble lie' by living according to an unjustified moral system rather than living in a way that is consistent with their naturalistic, evolutionary views.[12] For example, philosophy professor Joel Marks now believes that atheism implies that right and wrong do not exist. So those who believe in God are correct that without God no morality exists, but they are incorrect to believe God exists. If a greater being who issues commands does not exist, then those commands do not exist; hence, morality does not exist. He calls this 'hard atheism' in contrast to the 'soft atheism' of Dawkins and his fellow new atheists. He also argues that human beings can still discover many naturally explainable internal resources for motivating certain preferences. His project is to try to reduce animal suffering and exploitation.[13] Although such a project might bring a sense of satisfaction that

---

12. Poythress, *Richard Dawkins*, pp. 119-125.
13. Joel Marks, 'An Amoral Manifesto (Part 1)', accessed at https://philosophynow.org/issues/80/An_Amoral_Manifesto_Part_I

something good is being accomplished, it is merely a personal preference, and we are all free to choose our own personal preferences. If right or wrong do not exist, then life is ultimately meaningless (called nihilism). Dawkins himself at one point recognizes the implications of a naturalistic view:

> ... if the universe were just electrons and selfish genes, meaningless tragedies ... are exactly what we would expect, along with equally meaningless *good* fortune. Such a universe would be neither evil nor good in its intention ... In a universe of blind physical forces and genetic replication, some people are going to get hurt, other people are going to get lucky, and you won't find any rhyme or reason in it, nor any justice. The universe we observe has precisely the properties we should expect if there is at bottom, no design, no purpose, no evil, and no good, nothing but blind pitiless indifference ... DNA neither knows nor cares. DNA just is. And we dance to its music.[14]

A natural approach to ethics that only acknowledges the existence of matter leads to moral subjectivism at best, and moral nihilism at worst.[15] Morality is not conditioned on anything other than our desires and values. In other

---

14. Richard Dawkins, *River Out of Eden: A Darwinian View of Life* (New York: Basic Books, 1995), pp. 132-3.
15. The following paragraphs are indebted to Stokes, *How to Be an Atheist*, pp. 217-241.

words, the source of what is valuable is what we think is valuable. If we are the source of values, then what is moral is a matter of our preferences. We may impose rules on ourselves and others, but they are not binding on anyone but are only a matter of taste.

Even though moral nihilism is a consistent conclusion of a naturalistic approach, it is a minority view among atheists. Very few atheists consistently live as if there is no right and wrong, or no right answers to solve moral disputes.[16] Moral nihilism is disturbing because it makes it hard to condemn the actions of serial killers like Ted Bundy and Jeffrey Dahmer. Nihilism is not an easy position to rally around. It is not that nihilism implies that we ought to murder, rape, and pillage; rather, it says nothing about what we should do in a moral sense. Human beings, however, are very committed to live in a way that expresses a moral commitment. It is ingrained in us. Although many atheists may have a benevolent attitude that seeks the good of others apart from a belief in God, such benevolence has no compelling or binding

---

16. An exception to this would be Alex Rosenberg, *The Atheist's Guide to Reality: Enjoying Life Without Illusions* (New York: W. W. Norton and Co., 2011). He argues that we need to face the fact that nihilism is true (p. 95). He writes, 'Our core morality isn't true, right, correct, and neither is any other. Nature just seduced us into thinking it's right ... our believing in its truth increases our individual genetic fitness' (p. 109). We should be moral because it makes us feel better than being immoral (p. 3).

claim on others, but is an arbitrary, subjective personal preference.[17] Natural selection has an amoral foundation. It can describe what is, but it cannot prescribe what ought to be done. Nothing that allows the fit to survive can be condemned as immoral. The fact that someone is human carries no moral weight. In other words, the weak have no legitimate recourse to appeal to principles of justice because principles of justice do not exist in a world of 'no design, no purpose, no evil, and no good'. In a world where tragedies are meaningless, there is no basis for moral outrage when a young child is horribly abused leading to her death. Human outrage has no moral basis in an amoral world. Rather, we experience moral outrage because we are made in the image of a God of justice who has established basic principles of right and wrong.

THE JUSTICE OF GOD

The word 'justice' brings us into a courtroom where a judge decides the guilt or innocence of those who come before him. A judge declares someone guilty or innocent based on an examination of the conduct of a person in relationship to the law. If a person has broken the law, then

---

17. Christian Smith, *Atheist Overreach: What Atheism Can't Deliver* (Oxford: Oxford University Press, 2019), pp. 45-9. He argues that there is no compelling reason to believe in a universal obligation to promote the good of all human beings based on the naturalistic premises of atheists (pp. 18, 23).

they are declared guilty. If a person has not broken the law, then they are declared innocent. Scripture presents God as the Judge of all the earth (Gen. 18:25) before whom every human being will one day give an account of the life that they have lived (2 Cor. 5:10). The basis of God's judgment is His law which is an expression of His righteous character. God will declare us as either guilty because we have broken His law, or righteous, because we have kept His law. He will reward the righteous who have kept the law and will punish the wicked who have broken the law. The possibility of standing before the Judge of all the earth to give an account of your life is a terrifying prospect, but, in the total picture, God's justice should bring comfort. It guarantees that the wrongs of this life will be made right, and it is the basis for God to accomplish His plan of salvation.

FULL JUSTICE DELAYED

God's justice cannot be separated from His holiness (see Chapter 2). God is not only the majestic transcendent God of creation, but all moral excellency is found in Him. His holiness demands that justice be established to set wrongs right and to render decisions against those who break His law. His justice also cannot be separated from His goodness (see Chapter 1). If God provides everything that is good for us, then we can be confident that He will govern the world righteously and will eventually establish justice in the world He has created. However, we should not expect that His full justice will be manifested in this life. The kingdom of God, which represents the rule of God, was established by Christ during His life on earth. The fullness of that kingdom will not be displayed until Christ comes again. During this age His kingdom is a spiritual kingdom that is advancing by the proclamation of the good news of the gospel as people believe in what Christ has accomplished for their salvation. This kingdom advances 'behind the scenes' but it will one day be revealed in all its glory. This kingdom is a kingdom of justice, but that justice will not be fully revealed until the coming of Christ. What this means is that God's full justice is delayed. We may experience in this life suffering, heartaches, and injustice committed against us. In some situations, like the horrible example of child abuse and murder that opened this chapter, it seems that there is very little that we can do to stop injustice. Perhaps the boyfriend who murdered the little girl will experience some consequences now for what he did, but the delay of justice can be painful. Knowing that one day God's justice will be revealed and that this man will have to give an account of what he has done before the holy Judge of all the earth should bring a sense of hope and longing for that day. The moral outrage we experience in this life will one day be satisfied because God's justice will be manifested.

The delay of God's justice does not mean that the world is morally out of control. In some situations, like the incident of child abuse and murder, and in some periods of history (Stalin and Hitler), it may appear that God is unconcerned about what is happening on earth. We cannot explain many things (Deut. 29:29), but we have confidence that the Judge of all the earth will do what is just (Gen. 18:25) and that He will one day make things right. In fact, He is at work in several ways now to restrain evil. God has not left creation to run on its own, but He preserves creation by 'upholding all things by the word of his power' (Heb. 1:3 KJV) and He rules over creation, including the actions of those He has created (Ps. 103:19).

GOD'S RESTRAINT OF EVIL

God restrains evil in this world in many ways. Built into creation is the principle that a person will reap what he or she sows. Proverbs 26:27 states, 'Whoever digs a pit will fall into it, and a stone will come back on him who starts it rolling'. This proverb expresses the idea that those who plan to harm others are many times caught in their own wrongdoing and experience what they hoped to inflict on others (for a good example of this read Esther 5:9-7:10).[18] This is very similar to the principle that people reap what they sow (Gal. 6:7). The latter proverb is broader than Prov. 26:27 because it deals with general behavior and not just behavior meant to harm others. Neither principle is automatic so that we should not judge that someone has done something wrong if they are having a hard time or are suffering in some way (John 9:1-3). But if a person is negative toward others, drinks too much alcohol or spends their money unwisely, we are not surprised that a person who lives in such a way may suffer financially or in other ways.

God also uses civil governments to restrain evil. Although no earthly civil government is perfect, the authority that civil magistrates exercise comes from God. They are even called 'God's servants' so that to resist such authorities is to resist what God has appointed (Rom. 13:1-4). Part of their role is to restrain evil by punishing those who break the law. We are also to pray for those who are in authority over us that through their governing we may lead a peaceful and quiet life (1 Tim. 2:1-7). One function of civil government is to keep the peace. Although any human institution can go wrong or have people who are 'bad apples', civil government is one way that God establishes justice in

---

18. Lindsay Wilson, *Proverbs: An Introduction and Commentary* (Grand Rapids: IVP Academic, 2018), p. 282.

this world. The delay of God's full justice does not mean that we are left on our own. God is at work in a variety of ways fulfilling His purposes.

A Failure of Justice?

Many times, however, justice is not carried out in these ways. What if the one who digs the pit does not fall into it? What if earthly judges fail to render just decisions or someone escapes the consequences of their actions? For example, Pol Pot was the communist leader who took over much of Cambodia, including the capital Phnom Penh, in 1975. It is estimated that by 1979 1.5 to 3 million people had been killed under his rule. Their bodies were dumped into mass graves called 'the killing fields'. These deaths were not quick deaths but were torturous deaths taking place over several days. With blood on his hands, he died in his sleep at the age of seventy-two never having to face the consequences of his actions.[19] Most people experience a sense of outrage that someone could be responsible for the deaths of millions and yet not face the consequences of his actions. We long for something more, for justice to right the wrongs of millions of lives taken without cause. There *is* something more – a coming day of judgment where people will stand before

---

19. Benjamin M. Skaug, *How Could a Loving God Send Anyone to Hell?* (Ross-shire: Christian Focus Publications, 2019), p. 16-18.

the righteous Judge and give an account of what they have done. Our only hope of wrongs being made right is that God will execute His perfect justice.

THE EXECUTION OF JUSTICE

Many people consider the execution of justice as something that is wrong or barbaric. But to someone who has suffered terrible injustice, the execution of justice is not barbaric. In fact, the application of the righteous standards of the law in blessing or punishment is an act of love. God's justice is not incompatible with His love. Scripture affirms that 'God is love' (1 John 4:8). His love is an essential attribute without which He would not be God.[20] It is not opposed to standards of righteousness. In fact, because God loves goodness, He hates evil. These two are opposite sides of the same coin. God's standard of righteousness is expressed in His law, summarized in the Ten Commandments. Any violation of God's law brings condemnation and the possibility of punishment (James 2:10). God Himself is angry at the evil plotting of the wicked (Ps. 7:11). He hates evildoers (Ps. 5:5) and promises one day to bring wickedness and injustice to an end. For God to establish goodness He must exercise His justice in the punishment of wickedness.

---

20. John M. Frame, *Systematic Theology: An Introduction to Christian Belief* (Phillipsburg: P&R Publishing, 2013), pp. 237, 272.

Sometimes God's anger is expressed as burning hot when He is particularly troubled by wickedness. The word 'wrath' is many times used for this stronger statement of God's anger and is used for a variety of situations. For example, it is expressed when those who are weak, such as the widow, fatherless and sojourner[21] are mistreated (Exod. 22:21-24). Even the disobedience of His own people can provoke His wrath (Deut. 9:7), especially when they engage in idolatry (Exod. 32:10; Jer. 44:8). Those who are the enemies of God (Ps. 21:8-9) and plot against Him (Ps. 2:5, 12) will not be successful but will experience His wrath. A day of the Lord is coming, a day of final judgment, which is also called a day of wrath (Isa. 13:9; Rev. 6:16-17) when everyone will give an account to God. This will take place at the second coming of Christ (Rev. 19:15) when the fullness of His kingdom will be established, and wickedness will receive its just reward.

Many people have trouble with the idea of the wrath of God toward sin. We sometimes judge God by how humans react to situations of injustice. Our reactions

---

21. A sojourner is a non-Israelite who has special status within the nation of Israel. Other foreigners can be charged interest by the Israelites, but a sojourner cannot be charged interest (Lev. 25:35-38; Deut. 15:3). A sojourner is vulnerable because he does not own land and is regularly mentioned with the widows and orphans as a group that must not be mistreated.

of rage are many times driven by our emotions and so we overreact to situations by proposing 'solutions' that have no objective standard of judgment. God's wrath is not like road rage where a person shoots someone for cutting them off in traffic or for going too slow. Human anger can be characterized by deep-seated resentment causing people to lash out at others.[22] People have short fuses. God's reactions are governed by His character and His standards of justice. We are also blinded by our own corruptions. We do not understand the true nature of our hearts (Jer. 17:9). Imagine if a couple lovingly adopted an infant that faced certain death because it was left to die at the garbage dump. They love the child and raise him as their own. Even though this couple is very poor, they work hard and provide everything that the child needs to live a prosperous and productive life. Soon after their son graduates from college and has landed a job that pays several thousand dollars a year, he turns on them and murders them. During the trial he expresses that the reason he murdered his parents is that he did not want to be bothered with taking care of them in their old age. We would expect and hope that the judge would throw the book at this young man for not being grateful for parents who saved him from certain death and provided

22. William Edgar, *Does Christianity Really Work?* (Ross-shire: Christian Focus Publications, 2016), pp. 153-4.

everything he needed. We would be appalled if the judge gave him a light sentence. As hard as it is to think of ourselves as acting like this adopted son, we have all treated God this way. Although we cannot murder God, we can live in such a way that we ignore Him because deep down in our sinful hearts we despise Him.

The thought of standing before the Judge of all the earth to give an account of your life can be a terrifying thought. The final judgment is irreversible with your destiny hanging in the balance before a righteous Judge. God is a God of moral purity and expresses moral outrage at our sin. If we are honest with ourselves, we fall short of His standard of righteousness, which means that we will receive a sentence of condemnation. Because we are dead in our sins (Eph. 2:1-3), we are not able to do enough good to overcome the wicked character of our lives (Rom. 2:5-6, 15-16; 6:23). Don't fool yourself by applying a minimal standard which you think will make you look good before the law. Sin is not just related to our external actions but is a matter of the thoughts and intentions of our hearts (Jer. 17:9). Just as in a human court, one violation of the law can bring punishment, so in God's courtroom our violations of the law must be condemned. We stand no hope of acquittal based on our own actions and thoughts. We are like Baby Jessica, caught in a dark hole without the possibility of escape, unless someone with the ability and willingness to save us acts on our behalf (see the story at the beginning of Chapter 2).

The good news is that standing before the Judge of all the earth to give an account of our lives does not have to be terrifying. The justice of God can also bring great comfort. It ensures that people who have committed horrifying acts of cruelty against others will give an account to God on the Day of Judgment. A person like Pol Pot will face the consequences of what he has done. It gives a sense of assurance to those who have suffered greatly at the hands of others that a day of reckoning is coming. The justice of God can also bring great comfort to you if you recognize your wickedness before a holy God. Even though you deserve whatever sentence the just Judge would give to you, even separation from Him for all eternity, God can maintain His justice and wrath against sin, and declare that you are righteous before the law. Just to be clear, you are not righteous before the law, but God can declare you righteous before the law. How can He do that? You can be declared righteous before the law based on what Jesus has done in His life and in His death. Jesus lived a perfectly righteous life and fulfilled all the requirements of the law. He died on the cross to take upon Himself the penalty that you deserve because of your sin. Even though Jesus did not sin, He took upon

Himself the penalty for sin through His suffering and death on the cross. In this way, Jesus has satisfied the righteous requirement of God which can be credited to your account. In other words, when you stand before God the Judge, you can plead the life and death of Christ on your behalf. God can declare you righteous based on the righteousness of Christ. You can receive His righteousness stamped on your record of sin so that God does not see your sin, but He sees the righteousness of Christ on your behalf. What a comfort and joy to know that your sins do not stand against you because of Christ. If you trust what Christ has done for you and God the Judge declares you righteous, your relationship to God changes dramatically. You no longer relate to Him as Judge, but you become a child of God and He becomes a Father to you (Gal. 4:6-7). Some may struggle with the justice and wrath of God, but in His great love, He has made a way for sinners to become His family and to enjoy His presence for all eternity. God can save us, and He is willing to save us. As Paul states in Romans 11:33, 'Oh, the depth of the riches and wisdom and knowledge of God! How unsearchable are His judgments and how inscrutable His ways!'

SUMMARY OF MAIN POINTS

- Universal principles of right and wrong cannot be established based on a materialistic worldview.

- Without universal moral principles there is no basis to judge what is right and wrong.

- If there is no way to judge what is right and wrong, then life is meaningless, and morality becomes an arbitrary, subjective, personal preference.

- Moral outrage is common to human beings because we are made in the image of a God who is the source of universal principles of justice.

- God's justice can be terrifying because everyone has broken the law of God, but it can also be a great comfort because it guarantees that the wrongs of this life will be made right, and it is the basis for His plan of salvation.

- Although the full justice of God will not be established until Christ comes again, God is now at work in a variety of ways to restrain the evil that is in the world.

- The execution of God's justice, including expressions of His anger against wrongdoing, is compatible with His love and goodness.

- Standing before the God of justice at the end of your life to give an account to Him of your deeds of wickedness can be terrifying, but if you trust in Jesus Christ for salvation you can be declared righteous based on His life and death. You can become a part of God's family with God as your heavenly Father.

4

Is God a God of Genocide?
Examining 'Texts of Violence'

THE BASIC CHARGE AGAINST THE GOD OF THE
OLD TESTAMENT: A MORAL MONSTER

We now come to address some of the specific charges brought against God from the New Atheists. It has become common for atheists to impugn the character of the God of the Old Testament, even suggesting that He is a moral monster. Dawkins' description of the God of the Old Testament has become quite well-known:

> The God of the Old Testament is arguably the most unpleasant character in all of fiction: jealous and proud of it; a petty, unjust, unforgiving control freak; a vindictive, bloodthirsty ethnic cleanser; a misogynistic, homophobic, racist, infanticidal, genocidal, filicidal, pestilential, megalomaniac, sadomasochistic, capriciously malevolent bully.[1]

1. Dawkins, *The God Delusion*, p. 51.

The following chapters will deal with the charges against God of genocide, xenophobia, and megalomania, but it is helpful to first deal with a couple of general principles related to these charges. Based on the above quote, Dawkins has moral outrage concerning the character of God. But where does this moral outrage come from? What are the standards by which Dawkins is going to judge the God of the Old Testament? Suppose we agree with Dawkins and embrace a naturalistic, materialistic worldview with Darwinian evolution at the center of it. The result is that we have no moral grounds for condemning any of the actions of God. Naturalism cannot lead to universal moral principles that are binding on everyone (see Chapter 3). It can try to make a case for certain preferences, such as living in an altruistic way, but if someone chooses to live a different way, the only recourse is to try to force your preference on someone else. Dawkins' moral outrage comes from the fact that he is made in the image of God. He has a sense of deity even though he suppresses it (Rom. 1:18-21) and seeks to live in a way that denies God. We might say that Dawkins has to borrow funds from a Christian worldview to raise his moral objections in the first place. That said, even if Dawkins is being inconsistent with his own worldview, Christians still need to rebut the charge that the God of the Old Testament behaves immorally by their own (Christian) moral standards, and that is what I aim to do in this chapter.

Although Dawkins' argument against the God of the Old Testament sounds very persuasive on the surface, a close examination of his reasoning shows many problems. He argues that belief in God is a delusion, which he defines as a persistent belief held in the face of strong contradictory evidence.[2] He does not really engage the justification for the existence of God in any substantial way. An examination of his arguments shows that they are riddled with fallacies that rest on false or invalid assumptions. For example, he attacks people who adhere to Christianity rather than their arguments, as when he calls Mother Teresa a 'sanctimonious hypocrite'.[3] He rarely deals with contrary evidence and presents a belief in God or Christianity in the worst possible light. For example, he calls faith one of the world's greatest evils and compares it to the smallpox virus that needs to be eradicated.[4] He presents a caricature of the God of the Old Testament and ignores passages that contradict this caricature. He thus presents a picture of God that Christians do not

---

2. Dawkins, *The God Delusion*, p. 28.
3. Dawkins, *The God Delusion*, p. 330. See Ransom Poythress, *Richard Dawkins* (Phillipsburg: P&R Publishing, 2018), p. 34.
4. Dawkins, *The God Delusion*, p. 347.

recognize.[5] He also does not examine his foundational belief of a naturalistic, material world produced by Darwinian evolution. On that basis, he argues that many things are impossible, such as creative intelligence as an explanation for the design in the universe and God cannot exist because everything that exists must have a natural, material cause.[6] He begs the question by assuming what he is trying to prove. It will become apparent that he has not understood the God of the Old Testament nor the 'problem' passages to which he appeals as the basis for his view of God.

THE SPECIFIC CHARGE: THE OLD TESTAMENT GOD IS A VIOLENT GOD WHO COMMANDS GENOCIDE

Several passages in the Old Testament are used to bring this charge against God, but most of them are centered on the march of the Israelites toward the land of Canaan and their subsequent conquest of the land of Canaan. The so-called 'imprecatory' psalms are also considered problematic texts of violence. The scriptural evidence will be presented here so that we can interact with it.

THE EXTERMINATION OF THE CANAANITES

1) In Numbers 31, as Israel is traveling through the wilderness, God tells Moses to avenge the people of

---

5.   David Robertson, *The Dawkins Letters*, rev. ed. (Ross-shire: Christian Focus Publications, 2007), p. 45.

6.   Poythress, *Richard Dawkins*, p. 35.

Israel concerning the Midianites. Israel is to punish the Midianites because they tried to destroy Israel as they journeyed in the wilderness by deceiving and seducing them to worship their gods (Num. 25). Not only were they to kill all the males, but they were also 'to kill every male among the little ones' and to kill every woman who had experienced a sexual relationship (Num. 31:17).

2) The perspective of the book of Deuteronomy is that Israel is on the plains of Moab getting ready to cross the Jordan to take the land of Canaan. Moses renews God's covenant with the people and gives them the law again in prospect of living as a nation in the land. In chapter 20 He gives them laws of warfare where they are to treat differently a city that is far away (outside the land of Canaan) from a city that is in the land of Canaan. For cities outside the land, Israel is to offer peace but the cities in the land are to be destroyed. Specifically, 'you shall save alive nothing that breathes, but you shall devote them to complete destruction … as the LORD your God has commanded' (Deut. 20:16-17). The reason for this command is so that the people will not influence the Israelites to commit abominable practices and to worship their false gods (v. 18).

3) The account of the conquest in the book of Joshua shows how Israel sought to carry out the commands that God had given them.

   a) The city of Jericho was taken and both men and women, young and old, were devoted to destruction (Josh. 6:21).

   b) Israel killed all the inhabitants of Ai, both men and women (Josh. 8:24-25).

   c) In the conquest of southern Canaan, Israel conquered many cities and put to death their kings and all the people in the city (Josh. 10:1-43). Phrases such as 'every person was devoted to destruction' and 'he left none remaining' are used throughout the chapter. The summary of the chapter states, 'He left none remaining, but devoted to destruction all that breathed, just as the LORD God of Israel commanded' (Josh. 10:40).

   d) The same procedures and similar statements are made in the conquest of northern Canaan (Josh. 11:1-23).

4) The extermination of the Amalekites (1 Sam. 15) – God told Saul to destroy the Amalekites because of their earlier treatment of the Israelites as they journeyed in the wilderness toward Mt. Sinai:

Now go and strike Amalek and devote to destruction all that they have. Do not spare them, but kill both man and woman, child and infant, ox and sheep, camel, and donkey (1 Sam. 15:3).

THE IMPRECATORY (CURSING) PSALMS

The imprecatory psalms are psalms that curse the enemies of Israel, who are also the enemies of the psalmist. One of the most difficult imprecatory psalms is Psalm 137, particularly verses 8-9, which includes the following words in response to Babylon's destruction of Jerusalem:

> O daughter of Babylon, doomed to be destroyed,
> blessed shall he be who repays you with what you
>   have done to us!
> Blessed shall he be who takes your little ones and
>   dashes them against the rock!

Such passages lead Dawkins and others to claim that God is a genocidal, bloodthirsty ethnic cleanser who commands bloody massacres to be carried out with xenophobic relish.[7] This is a serious charge that needs to be answered. We will try to answer it by discussing various terms, ideas, and statements related to this charge as we try to get a more accurate and less polemical perspective on these texts of the Old Testament.

---

7.   Dawkins, *The God Delusion*, p. 280.

RESPONSES TO THE CHARGE THAT GOD IS BLOODTHIRSTY AND GENOCIDAL

A variety of reactions to these Old Testament texts will be given in the form of questions that will raise the problems that people have with these texts.

1) How can we follow a God who commands the extermination of innocent people, including children?

One assumes that a righteous God would not command the extermination of someone who is innocent. It is particularly troubling that children are included because they are viewed as the epitome of innocence. The term 'innocent' is appropriate to use for people in several contexts. In situations of war, non-combatant civilians are usually considered innocent bystanders. Children are considered innocent because they have not experienced much of life and so they live freely without being aware of the dangers of life. However, in a theological context when talking about a person's relationship with God, there is no one who is innocent before God. Everyone has been tainted by corruption, including children. Most parents know by experience that no matter how hard we try to teach our children to share, they regularly act selfishly to protect their toys. We have inherited a corrupt nature from Adam (see chapter 1) and very early in life we express that corrupt nature by our actions and attitudes. Every area of our lives is affected by corruption. Our hearts are spiritually dead (Eph. 2:1), 'deceitful above all things, and desperately sick' (Jer. 17:9). Our minds are blinded to the truth of the gospel (2 Cor. 4:4). Our wills are slaves to lawlessness (Rom. 6:19-20) and our feelings cannot be trusted (Rom. 7:5). The natural condition of human beings as corrupted by sin is true for everyone (Rom. 3:10-11). Although human beings can do good things from a human perspective, we are not basically good at the core of our being. Corruption is not a secondary part of our existence but is at the center of our humanity.

None of us can stand before God and be declared not guilty. God is the righteous Judge who must condemn those who have broken His law. The extermination of the Canaanites is the righteous judgment of God against guilty, corrupt sinners. God Himself confirms this when He explains to Abraham that his descendants will inherit the land of Canaan after God delivers them from Egypt and brings them back to the land. Several hundred years must pass because 'the iniquity of the Amorites is not yet complete' (Gen. 15:16). In other words, the people living in the land of Canaan are very corrupt and by the time God brings Israel back to the land of Canaan, their corruption will be evident. The passing of time shows God's forbearance with human corruption, but it also shows that at some point wickedness must be judged. It is hard for people today to get an idea of the corruption of the Canaanites. The Canaanite gods were fertility gods who engaged in sexual immorality among themselves (including incest with sisters). The three goddesses Astarte, Anath, and Asherah were principally concerned with sex and war. These goddesses of war have a thirst for blood, as recounted in the following description of Anath:

> The blood was so deep that she waded in it up to her knees – nay, up to her neck. Under her feet were human heads, above her human hands flew like locusts. In her sensuous delight she decorated herself with suspended heads while she attached hands to her girdle. Her joy at the butchery is described in even more sadistic language. 'Her liver swelled with laughter, her heart was full of joy, the liver of Anath [was full of] exultation (?).' Afterwards, Anath was 'satisfied' and washed her hands in human gore before proceeding to other occupations.[8]

As the goddesses of sex, they were depicted in ways that accentuated the female organs.

As sacred prostitutes, they were called 'holy' (*qudshu*). The Egyptian representations of 'the Holy One' show her facing forward as a naked woman in the prime of life, standing on a lion, with a lily in one hand and a serpent or two in the other.[9] The fertility of the earth

---

8. William Foxwell Albright, *Archaeology and the Religion of Israel* (Charles Village: John Hopkins Press, 1942), p. 77.

9. Ibid., pp. 75-6.

results from the sexual union of a male god and a female goddess, an incestuous sexual relationship in the Baal cult. The resulting union fertilizes the earth with rain. Their worshippers were encouraged to emulate and stimulate the gods by engaging in different types of sexual immorality as a part of temple prostitution.[10] In this way their desire for prosperity could be realized. The kinds of sexual activity the worshippers participated in included adultery, bestiality, and homosexual acts. These practices are mentioned in Leviticus 18:20-30 with a warning to Israel that they should not engage in such activity as people do in the land of Canaan. One can only imagine the impact such sexual immorality would have on the fabric of the culture. It was probably not much different than the city of Sodom where not even ten people were found who did what was right (Gen. 18:32). The house in which the visitors to the city stayed was surrounded by the men of the city 'both young and old, all the people to the last man' with the intent of homosexual gang rape (Gen. 19:4-8). The extent of corruption in the city of Sodom is a good way to think of the extent of corruption later in the land of Canaan.

Child sacrifice, a horrendous practice mentioned in Leviticus 18:21 that seeks to placate and win favor from

---

10. For the justification of temple prostitution see Richard Davidson, *Flame of Yahweh* (Peabody: Hendrickson Publishers, 2007), pp. 88-9.

the gods, adds to the picture of wickedness among the inhabitants of Canaan. Clear evidence of child sacrifice is found in the Phoenician city of Carthage from 750 to 146 B.C. Charred bones of sacrificial victims, which included the bones of animals and young children, were discovered at a cemetery. The Phoenicians were of Canaanite ancestry and worshipped the god Baal Hammon, the patriarch of the Phoenician pantheon and the consort of Tanit, who was the chief Phoenician goddess at Carthage. The god Baal was a prominent god in the land of Canaan. The port city of Carthage was established in the eighth century on the northern border of Israel.[11] It is not surprising that earlier texts of Leviticus 18:21 and Deuteronomy 12:31 warned Israel against the practice of child sacrifice in the land of Canaan before Israel entered the land around 1400 B.C.[12] Sadly, evidence of child sacrifice exists after the conquest of the land of Canaan in an incident with the king of Moab (2 Kings 3:21-27) and among the kings of Israel (2 Kings 21:6; 23:10; Jer. 32:35). One result of not driving out the Canaanites from the land

---

11. Lawrence E. Stager and Samuel R. Wolff, 'Child Sacrifice at Carthage – Religious Rite or Population Control?' *BAR* 10.1 (January/February 1984), pp. 34-6.

12. Some Biblical scholars would argue that Israel entered the land around 1200, but either date makes the point that child sacrifice was already in the land of Canaan at an earlier date.

was that the Israelites themselves took up this wicked practice.

The method of sacrificing children was to burn the child in the fire. Deuteronomy 12:31 states that 'they even burn their sons and daughters in the fire to their gods'. Another way to express this practice is 'to cause the children to pass through the fire' (Lev. 18:21, 2 Kings 23:10, and Jer. 7:31), with many English translations translating the phrase 'to offer them to Molech' (NASB). The Greek author Kleitarchos (third century B.C.) was paraphrased by a later author as describing the practice in this way:

> Out of reverence for Kronos [the Greek equivalent of Baal Hammon], the Phoenicians, and especially the Carthaginians, whenever they seek to obtain some great favor, vow one of their children, burning it as a sacrifice to the deity, if they are especially eager to gain success. There stands in the midst a bronze statue of Kronos, its hands extended over a bronze brazier, the flames of which engulf the child.[13]

This practice is considered extremely evil to the God of Israel. It is called an abomination that the LORD hates (Deut. 12:31). God hates this practice for several reasons. First, it is the useless taking of human life. People offer children as sacrifices to try to win favor from the gods so they will bless them in some way. But these gods are false

---

13. Ibid., pp. 32-3.

gods that do not exist. The people are praying to a figment of their imagination hoping to win favor from something that is non-existent. The sacrificing of children to such gods is totally useless. Secondly, these children are made in the image of God and so to sacrifice them to false gods is murder because in God's eyes it is the unlawful taking of human life. And finally, God is the creator and author of life and only He has the authority over life and death, including the death of children. When God made Adam, He breathed into his nostrils the breath of life (Gen. 2:7). God is the fountain of life (Ps. 36:9) because He is the source of life. When Job lost most of his possessions, and his children, he responded with the following words,

> Naked I came from my mother's womb, and naked shall I return. The LORD gave and the LORD has taken away; blessed be the name of the LORD (Job 1:21).

Job acknowledges that we enter this world with nothing and that we leave this world with nothing. Everything that we receive in this world is a gift from God, including our lives and the lives of our children. The tree of life in the Garden of Eden (Gen. 2:9) sums up the fullness of life because it includes not only physical life but spiritual life.[14] If God is the sovereign Creator of all life and has the right to govern the

---

14. John Frame, *The Doctrine of the Christian Life* (Phillipsburg: P&R Publishing, 2008), p. 684.

universe which He has made, then no one can hinder His purposes or challenge His actions (Dan. 4:35). God does all that He pleases (Ps. 115:3), working out all things according to His purposes (Eph. 1:11). As the potter has power over the clay, God can make out of the same lump of clay a vessel for honorable use and another vessel for dishonorable use (Rom. 9:21). As the author of life, God has the authority to take life according to His sovereign purposes. But even as He exercises this authority, He is patient (Gen. 15:14-16), slow to anger, abounding in steadfast love (Exod. 34:6-7). The possibility of the destruction of most of humanity before the Flood brought grief to God (Gen. 6:6). God takes no pleasure in the death of the wicked (Ezek. 18:23).

Passages in the Old Testament that describe the destruction of human beings, including women and children, are in the context of the execution of God's judgment against persistent or horrendous deeds of wickedness. The Amalekites took advantage of the Israelites as they journeyed from Egypt to Mt. Sinai. They attacked those who lagged behind because they were faint and weary. In other words, they destroyed those who were the weakest and most vulnerable. No doubt children were in this group. They showed no fear of God in this attack. The Israelites are commanded by God to blot out the memory of Amalek after they have taken the land of Canaan (Deut. 25:17-19). The psalms of cursing arose out of situations of betrayal or devastation where life had been turned upside down by the wickedness of others. In Psalm 137 the people have lost everything, including their homes and their temple, and have been taken to a foreign land. The Babylonians had besieged the city of Jerusalem, cutting off all supplies to the city, so that the people had to resort to cannibalism (Lam. 4:10). When the siege ended, the city and temple were destroyed and many Jewish people, including sons and daughters, were slain in the process. The concern of Psalm 137 is not personal revenge against the Babylonians, but concern for Jerusalem, which stands for the kingdom and purposes of God. The psalmist even offers a self-curse if he should ever forget Jerusalem and not set the cause of God as his highest joy (vv. 5-6). The psalmist asks God to remember the Edomites (v. 7), descendants of Esau and blood brothers to Israel, because of their treasonous acts of violence when Jerusalem fell. The curse against Babylon is asking for justice in the form of retribution so that what the Babylonians did to Israel will in turn happen to them (vv. 8-9). The statement about the destruction of the children of Babylon is a statement of faith in a prophecy of Isaiah who had prophesied the downfall of Babylon and the destruction of their infants (Isa. 13:16).[15]

---

15. For more on the psalms of cursing see Richard P. Belcher, Jr., *The Messiah and the Psalms* (Ross-shire: Christian Focus Publications, 2006), pp. 76-83 and the very helpful booklet by

The death of women and children in the destruction of the Canaanites is the most difficult thing for people to accept because it makes God look like a cruel despot. A summary of the argument to this point might help put things in perspective. First, no one is righteous before God. We have all sinned and fallen short of the glory of God (Rom. 3:23) and so we deserve His judgment for our wickedness (Rom. 3:9-20). God's justice must punish wickedness, but this is also good news, because God provides a way for His justice to be met and for us to be forgiven (see below). Second, the evidence of corruption is justified by our experience. We see the results in the actions of adults and children. We do not need to teach our children to selfishly guard their own toys because it comes naturally. We also experience corruption in the depths of our hearts. The point here is not that the Canaanite women and children were thoroughly evil. Rather, the point is that on the Christian view *all* humans are corrupted by sin and therefore deserve judgment from a holy God.

Third, in situations of the Old Testament where women and children are destroyed, God gave warnings about the coming judgment and was very long suffering with people by giving them every opportunity to repent (Gen. 15:12-16). In other words, the corruption of the

Sean McGowan, *Psalms That Curse: A Brief Primer* (White Rock: Reformation Zion Publishing, 2021).

people was evident and affected all of society. Fourth, in the destruction of the Canaanites, God was protecting His people from the corruption of the Canaanites so that they could fulfill the mission He had given to them (Deut. 12:29-31). Fifth, God is the author of life, and therefore He has the authority to take away life according to His purposes (Gen. 2:7; Ps. 36:9). Finally, the justice of God must be placed in the context of His abundant grace and mercy to people who reject Him even as He provides the very air that they breathe, and many other blessings that come in living in the world He has created. This issue brings us face to face with the holiness and justice of God (see Chapters 2 and 3). Will we bow before His authority or will we continue to reject Him even in the light of His goodness and grace?

Without a belief in God as the author of life, it is very difficult for any culture to maintain the sanctity of human life. Darwinian evolution affirms a naturalistic view of life that has no place for God. Natural selection and survival of the fittest does not distinguish between humans and animals. If humans are in the same category as the animal kingdom and the difference between the two is one of degree and not of kind, there is no basis to argue that humans should be treated any differently than animals. If that is the case, then why have a morality for humans that is different for animals, especially if morality itself is a product of evolution? We can be thankful that not everyone who believes in Darwinian evolution lives out these principles in a consistent way. However, one scholar has tried to consistently apply these principles in developing a quality-of-life view instead of a sanctity-of-life view. Peter Singer is professor of bioethics at Princeton University and is head of the Center for Human Values. The problem he has with the sanctity of life view is that it privileges human beings by assuming that one species is better than another species. This is 'speciesism' and is discriminatory because all species should be treated the same. The quality of life is based on the capacity of humans and animals to suffer. Suffering itself is dependent on the fact that humans and animals are self-conscious or self-aware beings. In fact, Singer argues that without consciousness or self-awareness, there is no personhood. This means that some humans are non-persons, and some nonhuman animals are persons. A preconscious human cannot suffer as much as a conscious horse and so the horse is more valuable. The prospect of suffering becomes the basis for evaluating the quality of life and making decisions about life itself. The implications are staggering. He argues that a newborn should not be considered a person until thirty days after the birth and that parents should be able to kill a child within that period if the child is going to suffer a lot (Downs Syndrome is used as an example).[16] Most would call this infanticide. Such a practice is consistent with Darwinian evolution where distinctions between humans and animals are blurred. Without a robust view of human beings made in the image of God, no reason exists to treat human beings differently than animals.

2) If God commanded the extermination of a group of people at one point of history, should we be concerned that He will command such action again, or that Christians today would follow the example of Old Testament Israel?

There are several reasons why this question is relevant to our discussion. Most modern people are aware of a particular religion that has advocated violence against those who reject their God. Although not all followers of Islam promote violence against infidels, too many examples exist of violent actions taken by radical Islamists against those who do not follow their God or who speak out against their God. The destruction of the World Trade Center towers in New York City on September 11, 2001, was orchestrated by Osama bin Laden, the founder of Al-Qaeda, as retaliation against the United States for

---

16. Peter Singer, *Practical Ethics* (Oxford: Oxford University Press, 1986); see also Donald De Marco and Benjamin Wiker, 'Peter Singer', in *Architects of the Culture of Death* (San Francisco: Ignatius Press, 2004), pp. 361-374.

support of Israel and involvement in the Middle East. Al-Qaeda thinks that all Westerners should be thrown out of Islamic states and that all Muslims around the world should fight a holy war against the United States and Israel. In January 2015 two French Muslim brothers gunned down eleven people at the offices of Charlie Hebdo, a publication that had printed several satirical cartoons over the years making fun of the prophet Muhammad. Their motive was to avenge the honor of their prophet. Some of the values of the modern West, including secularization, consumerism, materialism, the status of women, and sexual freedom, go against the grain of Islam's religion. All these bring the possibility of conflict and confrontation with radical Islamists.

Should people be concerned that Christians might take up the call to arms from Deuteronomy and Joshua to exterminate those who disagree with them? The answer is a resounding 'No'! The extermination of the Canaanites was a one-time unique event. In addition to the judgment of God against the wicked practices of the Canaanites, the land had been promised to Abraham's descendants by God and was necessary as a foundation for Israel to fulfill God's purposes to restore fallen humanity. Israel was to be a kingdom of priests (Exod. 19:6) to mediate the blessings of God to the nations. If Israel would trust God and be obedient, He promised that He would bless them abundantly so that the nations would see those blessings and desire to learn more about the great God that Israel served and the law He had given to them (Deut. 4:5-8, 28:1-14). King Solomon brought Israel to the height of her influence at the beginning of his reign. The kings of the nations and the Queen of Sheba came to Israel to see the great things that were taking place (1 Kings 1:37; 3:12-14; 4:20-21, 34; 10:1-5, 23-25). The sad thing is that Solomon's heart was turned away from the LORD by his foreign wives (1 Kings 11), which eventually led to the division of the kingdom (1 Kings 12). The history of Israel was a history of rebellion against God and eventually both the Northern Kingdom and the Southern Kingdom lost their land in exile. But never again in the history of Israel did God command Israel to go on the offensive and destroy people from other lands.

God remained faithful to His covenant promises and sent His own Son to do everything necessary to secure salvation. Jesus came as a suffering servant, a king who would lay down His life to pay for the penalty of sin. The kingdom that Jesus established is a spiritual kingdom that does not operate like an earthly, political kingdom (John 18:36). Those who become a part of Christ's kingdom by repenting of their sins and believing in His death as a sacrifice for their sin, do not advance His kingdom by physical warfare, conquest, or the use of violence. The spiritual kingdom of Christ is advanced by preaching the good news of salvation so that people can receive Him as their Savior and King (Matt. 28:19-20). The followers of Christ understand that just as Jesus was persecuted, so they may be persecuted, even to the point of death. Although His followers have not always been faithful to this mission,[17] church history is full of examples of those who were willing to die for Christ rather than deny Him. People should not be concerned about whether Christians might advance the kingdom of Christ through violence or putting people to death. The Holy Scriptures of the Old and New Testaments are complete,[18] so if anyone claims that God has told them to exterminate a group of people for whatever reason, they are liars and false prophets.

3) Shouldn't we follow Jesus who loves others rather than the violent God of the OT?

Many have drawn a distinction between the loving actions of Jesus and the violent actions of the God of the Old Testament to reject not only the violence of the Old Testament, but also the God of the Old Testament. For example:

---

17. See Mark Coppenger, *If Christianity Is So Good, Why Are Christians So Bad?* (Ross-shire: Christian Focus Publications, 2022).
18. See Timothy Paul Jones, *Why Should I Trust the Bible?* (Ross-shire: Christian Focus Publications, 2019).

> The God portrayed in the OT is full of fury against sinners, but the God incarnate in Jesus is not. Jesus introduced an entirely new way of looking at God. God does not hate sinners or despise foreigners; much less does He desire their annihilation.[19]

This author wants to redefine the God of the Old Testament to make Him more Christlike. He also calls some Old Testament texts pre-Christ, sub-Christ, and anti-Christ. Richard Dawkins, a well-known atheist, is not sure that Jesus existed, but he argues that from a moral point of view His teaching is a huge improvement over the cruel ogre of the God of the Old Testament. He calls Jesus one of the great ethical innovators and views the Sermon on the Mount as ahead of its time.[20] He even wrote an article entitled, 'Atheists for Jesus'.[21]

Although differences exist between the Old Testament and the New Testament, there is also a basic unity between the two. Jesus endorsed the Old Testament in several ways. He told two of His followers that they were slow of heart to believe all that the prophets had spoken

---

19. C. S. Cowles, 'The Case for Radical Discontinuity', in *Show Them No Mercy: Four Views on God and Canaanite Genocide*, ed. Stanley N. Gundry (Grand Rapids: Zondervan, 2003), p. 29.

20. Dawkins, *The God Delusion*, p. 283.

21. https://cdn.centerforinquiry.org/wp-content/uploads/sites/26/2005/01/22160306/p09.pdf. For some critical commentary on Dawkins's essay, see https://www.theolatte.com/2020/09/atheists-for-jesus.

(Luke 24:25). He affirmed all three sections of the Old Testament (the Law, the Prophets, and the Psalms) when He told His disciples that everything written about Him must be fulfilled (Luke 24:44). Jesus asked His Father to sanctify His disciples in the truth, and then stated, 'your word is truth'. The Word of God that existed at that time was the Old Testament. Jesus affirmed the authority and truth of the Old Testament for God's people. It is against Jesus' own view of the Old Testament for us to call it sub-Christ and anti-Christ.[22]

Jesus taught the disciples about the Father which can only be a reference to the God of the Old Testament. He told the disciples that He is 'your Father' and He called Him perfect (Matt. 5:48). He also highlighted the loving relationship that the disciples can have with the Father who supplies what they need (Matt. 6:7-13, 25-34), forgives them of their sins (Matt. 6:14), and rewards them (Matt. 6:2-4). This is a small sampling of the passages that describe the relationship of the disciples of Jesus with their Father, the God of the Old Testament. He is a loving father who will provide all that they need.

As the Son of God (Luke 3:22; Rom. 1:4), Jesus also had a close relationship to His Father. There are passages that speak of their unity of purpose which placed Jesus on

---

22. See John Wenham, *Christ and the Bible*, 3rd ed. (Eugene: Wipf & Stock Publishers, 2009), pp. 16-43.

the same level as His Father. For example, Jesus asserted, 'I and the Father are one' (John 10:30). The Jewish people understood that Jesus was claiming equality with God because they picked up stones to stone Him for blasphemy. They explained, 'you, being a man, make yourself God' (John 10:33). In John 5:17, Jesus placed His work on the same level as God's work. The Jews sought to kill Him because 'he was calling God his own Father, making himself equal with God' (John 5:18). Jesus identified Himself with God by using a name that is used for God in the Old Testament when He stated, 'before Abraham was, I am' (John 8:58). This is a reference to Exodus 3:14 where God identifies Himself to Moses as 'I AM WHO I AM'. Again, the Jewish people picked up stones to stone Him. If Jesus identified Himself with the God of the Old Testament, it would be hard for Him to have a negative view of that God!

Jesus also expressed a close relationship with His Father as He carried out His will to accomplish salvation. He expressed this in the Garden of Gethsemane when He wrestled with drinking the cup of God's wrath on behalf of sinners (Matt. 26:38-39). In His prayer to the Father before His arrest (John 17), He stated that He had accomplished all that His Father had sent Him to do. He also prayed that His present and future disciples would be kept from the evil one (John 17:15). Jesus willingly took upon Himself human nature to call a people to Himself and to offer His life as a sacrifice for their sin (Phil. 2:8). His work of suffering is in fulfillment of the Old Testament passages that speak of the coming of a suffering Servant (Ps. 22; Isa. 53). He willingly fulfilled the mission that His Father had given Him and so affirmed the character and purposes of the God of the Old Testament.

If one examines the life of Jesus, He was more than an ethical teacher. He was very compassionate toward sinners, but He was not always what our culture defines as nice. With a whip of cords, He drove the money changers out of the temple and overturned their tables because they had made God's house of prayer a den of robbers (Matt. 21:12-13; John 2:13-17). He condemned the religious leaders of His day, the scribes and Pharisees, for elevating their traditions above the law. Several times in Matthew 23 He called them hypocrites because they did not practice what they preached, and they kept people away from the kingdom of God rather than helping them to enter it. He called them blind guides (v. 16), whitewashed tombs (v. 27), sons of those who murdered the prophets (v. 31) and a brood of vipers who will not escape being sentenced to hell (v. 33). He pronounced judgment against them by declarations of 'Woe' (several times in Matthew 23). The Father had given such judgment to the Son (John 5:22) and Jesus declared that one day He will sit in judgment of all nations who will have to come before His throne (Matt. 25:31-32). One day every knee will bow before Him (Phil. 2:10). The book of Revelation presents Him as coming in judgment riding a white horse, His eyes like a flame of fire, clothed in a robe dipped in blood, and a sharp sword coming from His mouth to strike down the nations. He is King of kings and Lord of lords and will tread the winepress of the fury of the wrath of God, the Almighty (Rev. 19:11-16). He will defeat sin, Satan, and death to deliver His people. Hypocrites and those who are not ready for His coming will be consigned to that place where there will be weeping and gnashing of teeth (Matt. 24:51).[23]

Jesus is regarded by many non-Christians as a good moral person, but He did not regard the God of the Old Testament as behaving immorally. His teachings are in line with the God of the Old Testament, and He taught

---

23. If Jesus was a mere human being, then statements where He identified Himself with God or with the judge of all the earth are evidence of His delusions of grandeur. C. S. Lewis argues that if Jesus is a mere human being, then He is either a 'lunatic' or the 'Devil of Hell'. A mere man does not claim the things that Jesus claimed. You must either call Him a madman or 'fall at His feet and call Him Lord and God' (*Mere Christianity* [New York: Macmillan, 1960], pp. 55-6). Lewis, like millions of others, recognized Jesus as Lord and God.

His disciples that this God was their heavenly Father who would watch over them and care for them.

The coming judgment at the end of history is foreshadowed by the mission of Israel going into the land of Canaan to destroy the Canaanites. After God delivered His people from the bondage of Egypt, He established them as a kingdom over which He had absolute rule. God's holy presence dwelt in Israel so that nothing unholy or unclean could be allowed to dwell in His kingdom. Israel was to drive out and destroy the peoples living in Canaan to establish God's rule over the whole land in preparation for the glory of God to be displayed in Israel. This is a foreshadowing of God's judgment of unbelievers and the establishment of His rule over the new heavens and earth where nothing unclean will be allowed in His glorious presence (Rev. 21:5-8, 22:14-15).

PERSPECTIVES ON THE EXTERMINATION OF THE CANAANITES

This section will summarize the major points discussed in this chapter and draw some conclusions.

1) God is long suffering toward the wickedness of the Canaanites, but He is also a righteous Judge who will execute His justice against a very corrupt people (Gen. 15:16).

2) God is the Creator and author of life and has the authority to take life (Gen. 1:30, 2:7; Job 1:21).

3) It is a unique situation, even in the OT, that God directs Israel to destroy people living in a particular land so they could fulfill the mission God had given them.

Once Israel takes the land of Canaan, they do not engage in offensive warfare to take other lands. In other words, this is the only time in the Old Testament where God commands His people to take a land by destroying those living in the land. Deuteronomy 20 makes a distinction between the nations who are in the land and those who are outside the land. Nations outside the land can be offered terms of peace. God showed His approval of Israel taking the land by fighting on Israel's behalf when they fought against the kings who ruled in the land (Josh. 10-11). It is also significant that later in Israel's history, when Israel turned against God, that God fought against Israel, His own people (Jer. 21:5).

4) The church must not advance God's kingdom by the sword.

The mission of the church is to make disciples by teaching people the Word of God (Matt. 28:19-20). The church is not a nation state tied to one geographical area but has been sent out to the whole world. God's people today fight spiritual battles against spiritual forces of wickedness (Eph. 6:12). The church should never use force or physical violence to advance Christ's kingdom; rather, God's people follow the example of Christ by being willing to give their lives for the name of Christ.

5) The destruction of the Canaanites is a foreshadowing of the final judgment when God will destroy all those who have opposed Him and will vindicate those who have followed Him.

It is not accurate to call the destruction of the Canaanites an example of genocide or ethnic cleansing. The most important thing in the Old Testament is not your ethnicity but the God that you worship. Rahab, who lived in the city of Jericho, was spared when the city was destroyed because of her faith in Yahweh the God of Israel (Josh. 2:8-14; 6:25). Ruth was a Moabite who made a commitment to Yahweh, the God of Israel, and was fully accepted into the nation of Israel. In fact, both of these women even became part of the line of King David, and thus, also, the line of Christ.

The character of God as a God of justice should bring great comfort to those who have experienced genocide. In fact, such experiences have shown the necessity of God's justice. Here is an account of a person who experienced the horrors of war and the destruction of his people and villages:

> I used to think that wrath was unworthy of God. Isn't God love? Shouldn't divine love be beyond wrath? God is love, and God loves every person and every creature. That is exactly why God is wrathful against some of them. My last resistance to the idea of God's wrath was a casualty of the war in the former Yugoslavia, the region from which I come. According to some estimates, 200,000 people were killed and over 3,000,000 were displaced. *My* villages and cities were destroyed, *my* people shelled day in and day out, some of them brutalized beyond imagination, and I could not imagine God not being angry ... Though I used to complain about the indecency of the idea of God's wrath, I came to think that I would have to rebel against a God who *wasn't* wrathful at the sight of the world's evil. God isn't wrathful in spite of being love. God is wrathful because God is love.[24]

People who have experienced genocide and brutal injustice cannot imagine God not being angry against such evil acts. If God is not a God of justice, then the people who have committed such wicked deeds will never be brought to justice. Those who have suffered brutality would have no hope of things being made right. We long for justice because we are made in the image of the God who is a God of justice.

If we are honest with ourselves, we should also be concerned about standing before the holy God of justice to

---

24. Miroslav Volf, *Free of Charge: Giving and Forgiving in a Culture Stripped of Grace* (Grand Rapids: Zondervan, 2005), pp. 138-9.

give an account of our lives. Scripture is clear that all have sinned and fallen short of God's standard of righteousness. None are righteous before God. We all are responsible for paying the penalty for our wicked thoughts, actions, and feelings. We are by nature children of wrath and doomed to destruction, except for the great mercy of God which has provided a way of salvation for unworthy sinners. God has provided a way to declare us righteous even though we are not righteous by accepting in our place the righteousness of Jesus Christ. He fulfilled the law on our behalf and paid the penalty for our sin by dying on the cross. We who believe in Jesus receive His righteousness imputed to our account so that God no longer sees our sin but sees the righteousness of Christ. In this way, God's justice is satisfied, and He can declare us righteous. Our lives will never be the same because we no longer relate to God as Judge, but as our Father. Instead of being dead in our sins we are made alive to God and begin to see our lives changed by the power of His Holy Spirit. We no longer need to fear the great day of judgment because we are secure in the righteousness of Christ and we long to see our Father in heaven who has provided everything we need for this life and for the life to come. If you are unsure of your standing before a holy God, trust in Christ who has died on the cross to pay the penalty for your sin. Receive His grace and rest in His love. Your life will never be the same.

SUMMARY OF MAIN POINTS

- The charge that the God of the Old Testament is a moral monster is a caricature of God that ignores passages that contradict this caricature and so it presents God in the worst possible light.

- God's command to exterminate the Canaanites, including women and children, is the righteous judgment of God against a very wicked group of people whom God had been patient with for several hundred years. It is also important to recognize that God is the author and source of life so that He has the authority to take life according to His sovereign purposes.

- Without a belief in God as the author of life, and in human beings as made in His image, there is no basis to argue that humans are any different from animals, which can lead to treating animals better than human beings.

- People today should not fear that Christians will try to exterminate groups of people, because Christ established a spiritual kingdom through His death and resurrection that advances by preaching the good news of the gospel and not through conquest.

- Jesus affirmed both the Old Testament and the God of the Old Testament in His teachings and in His fulfillment of the mission God had given to Him.

• God's justice is a great comfort to those who have experienced the evil of genocide because it assures them that those who have committed such evil will be brought to justice.

• God's justice is a great comfort to all of us as sinners who are under his condemnation because it is by his justice that He can declare sinners righteous on the basis of the righteousness of Jesus Christ.

5

Is God a Cruel God?
Examining 'Texts of Oppression'

THE CHARGES AGAINST GOD

Richard Dawkins highlights this charge against God when he calls God 'a misogynistic, homophobic, racist' who is 'a capriciously malevolent bully'.[1] If God is a misogynistic God, then He is a God who hates women. Some texts of the Old Testament seem to be oppressive to women. For example, women are offered for sexual abuse to spare male visitors in the city of Sodom (Gen. 19:4-11; also Judg. 19:22-30). Some laws of the Old Testament seem to be detrimental to women.

If God is a racist God, then He must hate certain groups of people and so allowed His people Israel to show hatred toward them. This would explain why the Old Testament seems to support slavery and the bad treatment

---

1.   Dawkins, *The God Delusion*, p. 51.

of foreigners. If God supports the subjugation of other people, then the charge that God is a malevolent bully would seem to be confirmed. Some even argue that 'love thy neighbor' in both the Old and New Testaments really meant love only other Jews.[2] These charges against God are serious charges so we need to examine the Old Testament to see if God is a cruel God who supports the oppression of other people.

OLD TESTAMENT LAWS RELATED TO WOMEN

If someone is willing to take a fair look at the Old Testament within the historical context in which it was written, the conclusion will be that these charges against God are false charges and that the Old Testament is more humane and protective of people than any other writing of the ancient Near East. We will demonstrate this conclusion by examining texts of the Old Testament.

GOD'S AFFIRMATION OF WOMEN

As with most issues in the Bible, it is good to start with Genesis 1–2 to see God's design for His creation. God created men and women in His image, blessed both, and gave them the charge to be fruitful, to fill the earth, and to rule over it (Gen. 1:26-27). God created Adam first, but something (or someone) was missing in his life. It was not

---

2.   Ibid., pp. 287-8.

good that Adam was alone, so God made a helper suitable for him. The word 'helper' is a strong word that is used of God in other places in the Bible (Exod. 18:4; Ps. 33:20). The help that the woman brings to the relationship is essential to the work that God gave them to do. She is not inferior but is the perfect match (Gen. 2:23). The conclusion to this account is an affirmation of marriage: 'a man shall leave his father and his mother and hold fast to his wife, and they shall become one flesh' (Gen. 2:24).

Adam also has a representative role in the early chapters of Genesis. The Hebrew word *'ādām* is both a personal name, Adam, but is also the generic term for mankind (both male and female). Adam acts as a representative for his descendants and for his wife. Although each had to take responsibility for their disobedience, God addressed Adam first, even though Eve was first to disobey God by eating the fruit of the tree of knowledge of good and evil (Gen. 3:6). Adam also named his wife Eve because she was the mother of all living (Gen. 3:20). God's design was for the man and the woman to work together to accomplish their God-given mandate as each fulfilled their distinctive roles.

Adam and Eve's rebellion against God did not remove the work He had given them to do, but it made it much harder to accomplish. They had great obstacles to overcome. Work and childbirth would now be difficult. The marriage relationship would no longer be harmonious as it was before but would now be a place of conflict (Gen. 3:16-19). The consequences of wickedness change everything and open the door to the spread of attitudes and actions that go against God's designs. By the end of Genesis 4 there is polygamy and an attitude of revenge. It is no surprise to find within Scripture stories that describe acts of evil against women and others because of the spread of wickedness. The Bible is very honest about the condition of human beings and the horrendous acts that people do. It is imperative, however, to recognize that just because a story of wickedness is told in the Bible it does not mean that the Bible is endorsing the wicked actions. The story of the wickedness of Sodom is told to justify the judgment of God against that city. The similar story of the Levite and his concubine in Judges 19 is to show how wicked God's people had become during the days of the judges. What we will see in many of the laws in the Old Testament is that God is regulating situations brought about by the evil actions of people, to protect those who are vulnerable. We must recognize that many laws in the cultural context of the Old Testament have social practices that are foreign to us and can easily be misunderstood. Not all of the many laws in the Old Testament can be examined. We will look at a few representative examples.

THE LAW OF THE JEALOUS HUSBAND

This law in Numbers 5:17-31 addresses the concern a husband might have about his wife's faithfulness to the marriage. Two situations are in view. It is possible that the husband's jealousy is justified because his wife has had a sexual relationship with another man, and no one knows about it. Although her actions are undetected, she is impure because of her unfaithfulness. It is also possible that the husband's jealousy has no basis because the wife has not been unfaithful. In either situation, a process must be followed to determine the outcome.

One might conclude from a casual reading of the text that the deck is stacked against the wife. She is the one who is being accused. She is the one who must go through the process to determine her guilt or innocence. The priest sets her before the Lord, the hair of the woman is unbound, a grain offering is placed in her hands, and she is required to take an oath of her innocence. She is then made to drink the 'water of bitterness that brings a curse' (Num. 5:18). This drink is water mixed with dust from the tabernacle floor. If she has lied under oath, a curse will fall upon her that will result in her womb swelling and her thigh falling away (Num. 5:21-22). In other words, she will not be able to conceive children.

A closer look at this law will show that many protections for the woman are built into the law. This ordeal is much more humane and less dangerous than similar ordeals in the Ancient Near East. In the first ten chapters of Numbers, Israel is getting ready to leave Mt. Sinai and head to the Promised Land. As they move out, they must be pure as a nation to fulfill their mission. Specifically, chapters 5-6 address the importance of Israel being holy before God. Many of the situations mentioned in this section have already been covered in Leviticus. The camp itself must be purified because God dwells among the people (5:1-4). Debts must be repaid, including restitution to the Lord when a wrong is committed in relation to an offering brought to Him (5:5-10). In Numbers 6 a person may take a special vow to the Lord, called a Nazirite vow, and undergo certain restrictions to their lives to attain the level of the holiness of a priest. In the middle of these laws is the law of the jealous husband (5:11-31). Although the law of the jealous husband focuses on the wife, the other laws include both men and women. A woman can take the special vow to become a Nazirite because holiness is not limited to men but included women.

The law of the jealous husband addressed a particular problem that must have arisen in Israel where husbands became jealous of their wives and were suspicious that they had been unfaithful to the marriage covenant. A jealous husband could respond in many negative ways toward his wife that could be detrimental to her.

This law is meant to protect the wife from such abuse. A husband cannot blame or mistreat his wife based on suspicion alone. Evidence of unfaithfulness must be shown and the process in Numbers 5 puts the matter into the hands of God to decide.

First, the woman is brought to the priest, and she is presented to the Lord. Everything is done in the presence of God Himself. There are no grounds for anyone to dispute the result. If it is determined that the woman is innocent, the husband will have to accept this judgment and put away his jealousy. If it is determined that the woman is guilty of unfaithfulness, then she will have to face the consequences of her actions.

Second, the water of bitterness that brings upon her the curse is harmless by itself. It is holy water because it is taken from a vessel in the tabernacle. Dust from the floor of the tabernacle and the curses written in a book are washed into the water. What the woman drinks will not cause her any harm. The oath that she takes to testify to her innocence is the important part of the ceremony and her guilt or innocence will be determined based on whether she is telling the truth to God. Similar 'ordeals' existed in the ancient Near East that were used to determine a person's guilt or innocence. An accused person is subjected to a test that is believed to be under divine control. Many of these tests contain elements that are dangerous or harmful to the person undergoing the ordeal. For example, two laws in the Code of Hammurabi would have the accused person thrown into the river.[3] A river is full of all kinds of dangers apart from whether someone can swim. Of course, if the person does not make it, this would be seen as a divine verdict of guilt. The elements used in Numbers 5 are harmless, which would reduce the anxiety level of the person being accused and would clearly leave the verdict to God alone (Num. 5:21).

Third, the end of this process results either in the barrenness of the woman or in her ability to conceive children. The effect of the curse on the woman if she is guilty is to make her thigh fall away and her body to swell (5:21). It is clear from verse 28 that if the woman is not guilty, she will be able to conceive children. So, the curse must speak about barrenness or the inability to physically have children. A common view is that the word 'thigh' is a polite way to refer to the womb and that the 'body' may be referring to internal organs related to childbearing. If the woman is guilty, she will bear her iniquity (5:31), a phrase that further underscores that the punishment is

3. Hammurabi was a king of the first Babylonian dynasty who reigned in the 1700s B.C. The two laws are numbers 2 and 132 (James B. Pritchard, ed., *Ancient Near Eastern Texts Relating to the Old Testament* [Third Edition with Supplement; Princeton: Princeton University Press, 1969], pp. 166, 171).

left to God. This is a protection for the woman because the community has no role in determining the punishment. A community decision in such a case could lead to the death penalty. A woman in this situation should never be punished based on suspicion alone.[4]

DOES A WOMAN HAVE TO MARRY HER RAPIST?

Deuteronomy 22:28-29 seems to imply that a woman who is raped must marry her rapist:

> If a man meets a virgin who is not betrothed, and seizes her and lies with her, and they are found, then the man who lay with her shall give to the father of the woman fifty shekels of silver, and she shall be his wife, because he has violated her. He may not divorce her all his days.

To understand any Old Testament law, it is imperative to understand it in the historical context in which it occurred; otherwise, we will read into the law our own practices concerning marriage and severely misunderstand the intent of the law. God's design for marriage is given in Genesis 2:24 and is confirmed by Jesus in Matthew 19:4-9 in accordance with the commandment 'You shall not commit adultery' (Exod. 20:14). Aside from the Ten Commandments, the laws of the Old Testament are case

---

4. Timothy R. Ashley, *The Book of Numbers* (Grand Rapids: Eerdmans, 1992), p. 135.

laws that seek to regulate situations that might arise in Israel. A proper understanding of the case laws shows that part of their purpose is to protect the vulnerable of society.

Deuteronomy 22:28-29 occurs in a series of laws that deal with similar but different circumstances (Deut. 22:22-29). In 22:22 the simple case of adultery is examined where a man is found lying with another man's wife. This is a violation of God's law that has consequences not only for the man and the woman who are guilty of breaking the law, but also for the nation if the evil is not purged from the community. The result is that both the man and the woman must be put to death. In our individualistic cultural context, it is hard for us to see how adultery ripped apart the fabric of the relations in the community, brought irreparable damage to the families involved, and brought the possibility of God's judgment. Israel was a theocracy that enforced its own civil laws, religious laws, and moral laws. The church today is not a theocracy, has no power to put anyone to death, and does not advocate putting people to death for adultery. Instead, the church handles adultery by seeking repentance from those involved so there can be forgiveness and the restoration of relationships. Members of the church who do not repent could be liable to stronger measures of church discipline. The principle in the New Testament is the same as in the Old Testament: the congregation of God's people must be a holy community (1 Cor. 5:1-2).

The next two cases deal with a woman who is betrothed. The situation of betrothal is different from anything in our culture. It is not the same as being engaged because an engaged couple is not yet bound to the relationship in a legal way so that either the man or the woman can walk away from an engagement without penalty. A betrothed man and woman are considered married except that they have not yet consummated the marriage relationship. If sexual infidelity took place with a betrothed couple, a divorce was required to end the relationship and sometimes death would follow. In the first case described in 22:23-24 a man meets a betrothed virgin in the city and lies with her. Both are put to death; the woman because she did not cry out for help. The idea is that she is in the city and if she would have cried out for help someone would have heard her. The man is put to death because he violated his neighbor's wife by committing adultery with her. Notice that even though the woman was only betrothed, she was considered the wife of the man to whom she was betrothed.

In the second case of a woman who is betrothed (22:25-27), a man meets the woman in the open country and their sexual relationship is described as rape: the man seizes her and lies with her. The verb 'seize' (*ḥāzaq*) is used in other situations of the Old Testament to refer to rape (Judg. 19:25; 2 Sam. 13:11). The fact that this incident took place in the open country means that even if the girl cried out, there would be no one to help her. She is not guilty, but the man has committed an offense punishable by death because she was considered the wife of the man to whom she is betrothed.

The last case is an example of a man who meets a virgin who is not betrothed (22:28-29). He seizes her, lies with her, and they are discovered. Disagreement exists among commentators about whether these verses are describing rape; a case can be made that rape is not in view.[5] The verb translated 'seize' is not the verb used in rape cases (*ḥāzaq*) but is a different verb (*tāfash*). This verb is used in Isaiah 3:6 to take hold of someone to implore that person to be a leader and is also used to refer to Potiphar's wife when she seizes the garment of Joseph in her attempts to seduce him into a sexual relationship (Gen. 39:12). In describing the same situation of a man who lies with a virgin who is not betrothed, Exodus 22:16

---

5. Those who think rape is being described in Deut. 22:28-29, go on to explain how the law protects the woman who has been violated because the purity of the woman has been marred making it almost impossible for her to enjoy a normal marriage. Merrill comments that the perpetrator of the act must marry the girl (assuming her willingness) and could never divorce her (Eugene H. Merrill, *Deuteronomy* [Nashville: Broadman & Holman, Publishers, 1994], pp. 304-5).

uses the verb *pātāh* which means to persuade or seduce. Finally, although the verb *'innāh*, translated 'violate' in the ESV in Deuteronomy 22:29, is used in situations of rape (Judg. 19:24; 2 Sam. 13:12), it is also used in situations that do not involve rape to mean 'humiliate' (Deut. 21:14; 22:24).[6] The cases described in Deuteronomy 22:28-29 and Exodus 22:16-17 do not technically refer to rape but to a situation where the man persuaded the woman who is not betrothed to have a sexual relationship. In this case, the man shall give to the father of the young woman fifty shekels of silver, she shall become his wife, and he may never divorce her. The law in Exodus 22 adds that the money given to the father is the bride price and he must pay this price even if the father refuses to give his daughter to the man. Exodus 22:17 confirms that a woman is not required to marry a man who rapes her.

Several conclusions can be drawn from examining these laws. First, the Bible does not require a woman who is raped to marry her rapist. Those who try to argue against the morality of the Bible through memes that the Bible institutionalizes rape are severely misrepresenting what the Bible teaches. Distorting Scripture in this way is part of the shallow, cheap, sound bite world in which

---

6. For a perceptive article on these situations see Sandra L. Richter, 'Rape in Israel's World ... And Ours: A Study of Deuteronomy 22:23-29', *JETS* 64.1 (2021): pp. 62-75.

we live. Second, many don't understand how marriage works in the context of the Old Testament. The result is that the Old Testament laws are misunderstood and wrong conclusions are drawn that distort what the Old Testament is teaching. If people think being betrothed is the same thing as being engaged today, they will not understand what the Bible teaches in such situations. If people think being a single woman is better than being married, then they have not understood how marriage acts as a protection for women in that cultural context. If people think the commercial language in certain laws of the Old Testament treat women like property, then they have not understood the function of the bride price as economic protection for the woman. If people judge the marriage customs of the Old Testament by the modern standard of the moral autonomy of the individual, they will not understand the strong community ties that bind a person to the larger household. A household consisted of a single living male ancestor, his wife, the man's sons and their wives, grandsons and their wives, any unmarried male or female descendants, and any male or female hired servants and their families.[7] A person's legal status, whether male or female, was not determined

---

7. Daniel I. Block, 'Marriage and Family in Ancient Israel' in *Marriage and Family in the Biblical World*, ed. Ken M. Campbell (Downers Grove: InterVarsity Press, 2003), p. 38.

by an abstract universal notion of personhood but from an individual's position within the household.[8] One author asks a pertinent question, 'Shall we criticize the past for not being more modern and attempt to remake it in our own image?' After examining the laws of Deuteronomy 22:23-29, she makes several comments. Sexual boundaries in Israel were understood as guardrails that kept society from the abyss of delinquency, trauma, and economic ruin. Crimes in this area were crimes against the community. The legal system valued the well-being of its female citizens, empowered them with a voice in the courts, and based its decisions on civic authority and rational proof (not non-rational proofs like river ordeals). She also notes that in ancient Israel victims of sexual abuse were protected and rapists were prosecuted. She then concludes:

> I also must conclude, based on what I read in the constitution and bylaws of ancient Israel, that my daughters likely would have been safer wandering the hill country of Iron Age Israel than attempting to cross the quad at UCLA.[9]

It is also significant that the laws of Israel concerning sexual misconduct and rape are more humane than

---

8.   Richter, 'A Study of Deuteronomy 22:23-29', pp. 73-4.
9.   Ibid., pp. 75-6. UCLA is mentioned because of the way a rape case was handled there.

the laws of the ancient Near East. There are similar expectations concerning virginity, the bride price, a period of betrothal, the sanctity of marriage, and the importance of a woman's fertility for the benefit of the family.[10] The differences relate to the penalties that are enforced when a law in this area is violated. Examples from Mesopotamia include revenge rape (the wife of the perpetrator is raped), slave-concubinage for the rapist's wife, and the girl who was raped was expected to marry her rapist. The laws of Israel focus on maintaining the integrity of the covenant community by purging the evil from their midst. Such crimes were so serious that they would defile the land and lead to the judgment of exile (Lev. 18: 26-29; Deut. 32:45-47).[11]

CAPABLE WOMEN

The view that women in the Old Testament were the property of their fathers and husbands is a misconception and presents a false picture of the laws and the activities of women in the Old Testament.[12] Although the husband and father had a central role in Israelite society, the elevated status of the wife and mother of the household is

---

10. See Victor H. Matthews, 'Marriage and Family in the Ancient Near East' in *Marriage and Family in the Biblical World*, pp. 1-32.

11. Richter, 'Deuteronomy 22:23-29', pp. 69-71.

12. The following section is indebted to Block, 'Marriage and Family in Ancient Israel', pp. 66-7.

clearly presented in the Old Testament. Genesis 1 and 2 establish the equality of being a man and woman, and husband and wife, before God. Both are made in the image of God (1:27) and both are assigned the privilege and responsibility of governing the world (1:28). The woman, who is created to solve the problem of Adam's being alone, is not a servant who is below him but is a perfect complement to him (2:20-23). The mutuality of the marriage relationship is expressed in their unity of one flesh and in their mutual confidence and trust to stand naked before one another (2:24).

Although clear evidence of functional ordering exists in Genesis 1-2,[13] the emphasis is on the mutual relationship between husband and wife and that both are important for fulfilling the calling God gave to them. The entrance of sin in Genesis 3 distorts the relationship between the man and the woman and makes mutual dependence harder to live out (3:16), but it does not take away the responsibility to live according to God's original design. The rest of the Old Testament confirms this in many ways. First, it demonstrates the

---

13. Block mentions the following: God created man and woman consecutively, not simultaneously, God created woman to resolve a deficiency in the man's experience, God created woman from man, God presented the woman to the man, and the man named the woman ('Marriage and Family in Ancient Israel', p. 66).

importance of women and their influence in Israel. In the intimacy of marriage husbands and wives related to each other as equals (see the Song of Solomon). The fifth commandment shows that honor to both fathers and mothers is foundational to the community of Israel (Exod. 20:12). The teaching of the mother is emphasized along with the instruction of the father in relationship to the children (Prov. 1:8). The presentation of the excellent wife emphasizes her initiative, creativity, and energy as she works for the benefit of the family (Prov. 31:10-31). Many situations exist in the Old Testament where the wife exerts great influence over her husband (Gen. 16:1-6; 1 Sam. 1) and in some situations shows greater wisdom than her husband (1 Sam. 25). Second, those who were in leadership positions were to exercise their authority for the benefit of those they served, including kings (Deut.17:14-20), judges (Exod. 18:13-27), priests (Num. 6:24-27; Deut. 10:8-9), and prophets (Deut. 18:14-22). Third, many of the laws of the Old Testament were given to protect the vulnerable (Deut. 14:28-29).

The New Testament presents the same perspective of the equality and freedom of women in the context of servant leadership. Jesus treated women differently than many of the cultural expectations of the day. Women followed Him (Luke 8:1-3; Mark 15:41). He taught them (Luke 10:38-42; John 20:17). He spoke to the Samaritan woman at the well (John 4). He praised their faith (Matt. 15:21-28). He allowed Himself to be anointed by a woman who was a sinner while at the house of a Pharisee (Luke 7:36-50). Women were the first witnesses of His resurrection (Matt. 28:1-10; Luke 24:2-9). Although there are a few difficult texts in the letters of Paul (1 Cor. 11:2-16; 14:33-36), he also spoke of the freedom and equality of women. He affirmed that men and women do not differ in how they relate to God in salvation. Both men and women approach God through faith in Christ and both receive all the benefits of being in Christ (Gal. 3:28). He also commends the work of women by greeting them in some of his letters (Rom. 16:3, 6; Col. 4:15; 2 Tim. 4:21) and by highlighting their service (Rom. 16:1; Phil. 4:3).

SERVANT LEADERSHIP

Paul also developed further the idea of servant leadership in the context of marriage and the church. In marriage, the husband's role parallels the role of Christ in relationship to the church. Husbands are to love their wives as Christ loved the church. He demonstrated that love by putting the interests of the church before His own leading to His death. Husbands should love their wives in the same self-sacrificing way (Eph. 5:25-33). Paul demonstrated servant leadership in his service to the church. He consistently prayed for the churches and longed to see them (Rom. 1:9-11; Phil. 1:3-10). He carried the burdens of the churches and endured all kinds of hardships on their behalf (1 Cor. 4:11-13; 9:19; 2 Cor. 4:7-12, 16-18; 11:24-29). Paul's qualifications for elders exemplified the same spirit (1 Tim. 3:1-7; Titus 1:5-9). Peter exhorted the elders of the churches to demonstrate a self-giving spirit (1 Pet. 5:1-4).

OLD TESTAMENT LAWS RELATED TO THE VULNERABLE

This section addresses laws that seem to support the idea that God is a racist who hates certain groups of people and that He gives laws that oppress such groups. In other words, He is a malevolent bully. Laws will be examined related to slavery, foreigners, the sojourner, and the weak.

DOES THE OLD TESTAMENT SUPPORT CHATTEL SLAVERY?

English translations many times render the Hebrew word *'ebed* as 'slave'. When most people today hear the word slave, they think of chattel slavery where the slave is the legal property of another person. The slave is bound to absolute obedience because he is owned by his master. The slave has no rights, and the master can do with the slave whatever he wants. Slavery in the United Kingdom and the United States in the 1800s fits this definition. In addition, it targeted people of color from other parts of the world who were kidnapped and brought to the West. It was also a closed system with little opportunity to gain freedom. This type of slavery is not what is primarily in view in the laws of the Old Testament. In fact, several Old Testament laws legislate against chattel slavery. Both Exodus 21:16 and Deuteronomy 24:7 condemn stealing someone and selling him. Exodus 21:16 is a general statement that condemns the stealing, selling, and possession of another human being. Deuteronomy 24:7 is a specific statement related to the stealing and selling of a fellow Israelite. Both passages mandate the death penalty. Also, a runaway slave who made his way to Israel was not to be returned to his master but could live in one of the towns of Israel (Deut. 23:15). These laws undermine the institution of chattel slavery.

If chattel slavery is not what is in view, then what kind of servitude is described in the Old Testament laws? Indentured servitude is the best way to describe it. If someone became poor and could not pay his debts, several options were available to him.[14] He could sell some of his

---

14. Jay Sklar, *Leviticus: An Introduction and Commentary* (Downers Grove: IVP Academic, 2014), pp. 303-12 has a good discussion of the issues related to these laws.

land with the hope that a near relative, called a kinsman redeemer, would repurchase it for him to keep the wealth from the land in the family. Or perhaps the person who became poor could gain income from the rest of the land and buy back what he sold himself. If none of those options were available, the land would return to him in the Jubilee (Lev. 25:25-31). If a person had to sell all his property, fellow Israelites could loan him money without interest so he might make a living (Lev. 25:35-38), or the creditor could let him work the land as a tenant farmer to pay back his debt. The worst-case scenario would be if a person had to sell himself to pay off his debt. He would work for someone else until his debt was paid off or until the year of Jubilee when debts were released (Lev. 25:39-43). A person who fell into poverty became a hired worker to pay off his debts, and if he was not able to pay them off, he would be released from his debt and receive his land back in the Jubilee year.

It is easy to misunderstand Old Testament laws if the Hebrew word *'ebed* is consistently translated 'slave'. Although in some Old Testament passages the translation 'slave' is correct (Deut. 23:15), there are many passages where it gives the wrong impression. A better translation would be 'servant', 'hired-servant', or 'hired-worker' to describe an indentured servant. Leviticus 25:44-46 also speaks of permanent servants, a limited group in Israel who may be acquired from the nations or from non-Israelites who lived in the land. They are designated as property, a word that refers to what someone possesses, and may be part of the inheritance handed down to a son. It is important to understand that servants had legal rights in Israel. They were to rest on the Sabbath (Exod. 20:10) and went free if their masters abused them (Exod. 21:26-27). Plus, Israelite masters were commanded to treat their servants with compassion (Deut. 15:12-15; 16:11-12). The limited use of property language should not be understood as viewing servants as less than human. Property questions were central to many relationships in Israel because of the importance of inheritance. Commercial language is used of people today when we talk about what a free agent in baseball might be worth or when we transfer an employee to another location as one might transfer money.[15] When someone in Israel was facing poverty, becoming a servant brought certain benefits, such as regular food and shelter and a place in a stable family.[16] Although provisions were made for the poor, no welfare net existed to help people. Becoming an indentured servant could be a lifesaver.

---

15. These are examples of possession language that are weak. Strong possession language would emphasize that someone is my property and I can do with them as I wish.

16. Ibid., pp. 308-9.

DOES GOD HATE FOREIGNERS?

Some argue that the Israelites hated foreigners and mistreated outsiders who lived in Israel. Several Old Testament passages speak against certain nations, such as the Ammonites and the Moabites: 'No Ammonite or Moabite may enter the assembly of the LORD. Even to the tenth generation, none of them may enter the assembly of the LORD forever' (Deut. 23:3). Laws also exist that treat foreigners differently than Israelites, such as laws that allow for Israelites to charge interest to foreigners but not to fellow Israelites (Deut. 23:19-20). How are we to understand Israel's attitude to those who are non-Israelites? First, in every situation where negative comments occur about other nations or people groups, these comments are in response to some act of injustice or wickedness that had been committed by them. In the last chapter we saw that the negative statements about the Canaanites were in response to the wickedness of the Canaanites (Gen. 15:16; Lev. 18:25-28). The Ammonites and Moabites did not help the Israelites when they came out of Egypt, but, even more, they plotted to destroy them by hiring a diviner to curse them (Num. 22:1-6; 23-24). When that did not work, they enticed Israel to sin through false worship (Num. 25).

Second, more things are always going on in such statements than are evident in the passage itself. It is easy for people to cherry-pick a verse or two out of context to make it say something very negative toward God or Israel. One must not only look at a passage in its own context, but also know the stories and facts given in other places of Scripture to avoid drawing wrong conclusions. The Ammonites and Moabites are distant relatives of Israel who descended from Lot, the nephew of Abraham (Gen. 12:5). Their origin is described in Genesis 19. When Lot and his two daughters fled the destruction of Sodom, they took up residence in a cave because they were afraid to go to the city of Zoar. The daughters were concerned that they would not have the opportunity to produce children, so they came up with the plan to get their father drunk and to lie with him to 'preserve offspring from our father' (Gen. 19:32). The result of these incestuous relationships was the birth of Ammon and Moab, whose descendants were the Ammonites and Moabites. What makes their treatment of the Israelites more heinous is that they are related to Israel. What makes the statement against them about not being able to enter the assembly of the LORD so comprehensive is the incestuous beginning of each nation. Incestuous relationships among close family members were condemned in the law (Lev. 18:6-18). Knowledge of these facts is necessary to get a full understanding of Deuteronomy 23:3-6.

Third, the prohibition of the Ammonites and Moabites from entering the assembly of the LORD is not a prohibition from them entering the land of Israel. The phrase 'the assembly of the LORD' refers to specific gatherings within Israel devoted to religious purposes, such as worship and participation in the feasts. Even certain Israelites were prohibited from such gatherings if they were not in a state of cleanness. Deuteronomy mentions two situations that would keep anyone, including an Israelite, from the assembly (23:1-2). Someone who was emasculated would not meet the standard of wholeness required for worship (the priests and sacrificial animals also had to meet this standard). And yet, Isaiah 56 looks forward to a day when eunuchs will be part of the worshiping community. The work of Christ accomplished this because He fulfilled the requirements of what wholeness symbolized (perfection). People born from a forbidden union also could not enter the assembly of the LORD (v. 2). Such unions included Israelites marrying people who worshipped other gods and children born from temple prostitution and from incestuous relations. Even to the tenth generation none of the descendants of such a person could enter the assembly of the LORD. The word 'ten' was the number of completeness so this statement is emphasizing that this prohibition lasted forever (see also v. 3).[17] Also, no Moabite or Ammonite could enter the

---

17. John D. Currid, *Deuteronomy* (Darlington: Evangelical Press, 2006), p. 376.

assembly of the LORD to the tenth generation (vv. 3-6) because they did not show hospitality to Israel in the wilderness but plotted to seek Israel's destruction. An Edomite and an Egyptian were forbidden from entering the assembly until the third generation. The shorter length of time was because the Edomites were related to Israel (Edomites were descended from Esau, a brother of Jacob) and the Egyptians treated Israel well when they moved to Egypt during the time that Joseph was second in command to Pharaoh.

Fourth, whenever negative statements are made against other nations or people groups, the possibility of mercy always exists if a person is willing to commit to Yahweh, Israel's God. Rahab's family was saved when Jericho was destroyed because she believed in the God of Israel and helped the spies escape (Josh. 2:8-14; 6:22-25). Ruth was from Moab, but she also made a commitment to Yahweh when she accompanied Naomi back to Judah (Ruth 1:16-18). Ruth became a model of what it means to live a life of steadfast love (Ruth 2:11-12). She married a prominent citizen of Judah and through the son born to this marriage she became part of the line of David (Ruth 4:18-22). It is amazing that David, the great king of Israel who helped organize worship that would take place at the temple, was a descendant of a Moabite woman! Anyone under a curse, as in Deuteronomy 23, can find mercy if he or she seeks Yahweh in faith and repentance. The God of Israel is a gracious God who delights in showing mercy (Exod. 34:6-7). There is no comparison between His mercy and His justice. His justice toward the guilty extended to the third or fourth generation if there was no repentance, but His steadfast love cannot be exhausted as it extends to thousands upon thousands of generations.[18]

Fifth, the New Testament expands God's mercy to the nations through Christ's commission to His disciples to take the good news of the gospel to the whole world (Matt. 28:19-20). Gentiles do not have to become Jews to be part of Christ's kingdom. Rather, 'For God so loved the *world*, that he gave his only Son, that whoever believes in him should not perish but have eternal life' (John 3:16, emphasis added). The proper response is faith in Jesus Christ as the one who saves you from your sins, accompanied by repentance from sin. Anyone can receive Christ as their Savior, as Paul states in Galatians 3:28, 'There is neither Jew nor Greek, there is neither slave nor free, there is no male and female, for you are all one in Christ Jesus'. Christ has broken down the natural barriers that separate people so that unity can be experienced between different groups of people in

---

18. Duane A. Garrett, *A Commentary on Exodus* (Grand Rapids: Kregel Academic, 2014), p. 653.

Christ (Eph. 2:11-22). The goal of Israel to be a light to the nations (Isa. 49:6) is fulfilled in the mission of the church which is made up of people from every nation on earth (Rev. 7:9-10).

What about the treatment of the foreigners who lived in the nation of Israel? To answer this question, important distinctions must be made between non-Israelites who are sojourners and those who are foreigners. The sojourner (*gēr*) was someone who had abandoned their homeland for political or economic reasons and had sought refuge in Israel. They had special privileges because they were recognized by the host country. Non-Israelites who did not have these special privileges were usually in the country for business purposes or were traveling through the country with no intent of residing in the country. Common terms used to describe such people are 'foreigner' (*nekar*) or 'stranger' (*zār*).[19] Interest on a loan should not be charged to the sojourner (Lev. 25:35-37), but it could be charged to the foreigner (Deut. 15:3).[20] The sojourners had certain benefits that the foreigner did not have. Israel was commanded not

---

19. James K. Hoffmeier, *The Immigration Crisis: Immigrants, Aliens, and the Bible* (Wheaton: Crossway, 2009), pp. 50-3.

20. One problem in distinguishing sojourners from foreigners within Israel is that good English translations are not always consistent in the way they translate these different Hebrew words. For example, the word for 'sojourner' (*gēr*) in Lev. 25:35 is translated 'stranger' in the ESV.

to mistreat the sojourner (Exod. 22:21; 23:9). They were to be treated the same before the law as the Israelites (Exod. 12:49; Lev. 18:26). They could also enjoy certain religious benefits if they were circumcised, such as participation in the Passover and other religious festivals (Exod. 12:48; Lev. 16:29-30). They were placed in the same category as widows, the fatherless, and orphans (Lev. 19:9-10; 23:22; Deut. 24:19-22). They were to be treated with compassion because they were financially vulnerable. Israel had a place in her community for non-Israelites who wanted to live in Israel on a more permanent basis.

Based on the evidence of Scripture, God is not a racist who has animosity toward people who are not Jews. He treats different people groups within Israel with the respect they deserve as made in His image. He is also not a misogynist who hates women. The laws in the Old Testament have the purpose to protect the vulnerable. Both men and women have a major role to play in fulfilling God's purposes for the world. He is not a malevolent bully who seeks to oppress people who are outsiders. The acceptance of non-Israelite sojourners shows that love your neighbor was not limited to other Jews. Jesus' parable of the Good Samaritan makes this very point (Luke 10:25-37). If one approaches the Bible with an open mind to understand what Scripture is teaching, the charges brought against God by many today, including the new atheists, are seen to be superficial misunderstandings of His character.

SUMMARY OF MAIN POINTS

- The laws of the Old Testament are more human and protective of the vulnerable than any other laws of the Ancient Near East.

- The Bible honestly portrays the wicked actions of humans, including horrible actions of oppression, not to endorse such actions, but to justify the judgment of God.

- We must be sure we understand the cultural practices of the Ancient Near East, especially related to marriage, otherwise we will draw wrong conclusions from the laws related to marriage and sexuality.

- The Bible presents many examples of capable women who played key roles throughout redemptive history within the context of the servant leadership of men.

- The Bible does not support chattel slavery (the kind of slavery found in the UK and the USA); rather, there are laws in the Old Testament against it.

- The 'slavery' in the Old Testament is 'indentured servitude' where someone sells their labor to someone else to pay their debts.

- The God of the Old Testament does not hate foreigners as demonstrated in allowing foreigners, called sojourners, to come under the protection of the vulnerable in Israelite society and to allow non-Israelites to become full members of the community if they profess belief in the God of Israel (Rahab, Ruth).

- With the coming of Christ, the mission of the church, originally made up of Jewish people, was to take the good news of the gospel to every nation.

6

Is God a Megalomaniac? Examining 'Texts that Make Exclusive Claims'

THE CHARGES AGAINST GOD

A megalomaniac is a person who has an elevated view of his or her own importance or greatness. The term 'megalomania' can refer to a delusional mental illness that is marked by feelings of personal omnipotence and grandeur.[1] In other words, such people do not have a realistic or an appropriate view of their own place in the world and the level of their importance. They think more highly of themselves than they ought to think. Some might even have 'delusions of grandeur'.

God is charged with being a megalomaniac for several reasons. Dawkins calls God 'jealous and proud of it'. God's 'monumental rage' whenever His people

---

1. https://www.merriam-webster.com/dictionary/megalomaniac.

flirted with a rival god is an example of the worst kind of sexual jealousy.[2] God is a control freak, obsessed with His own superiority, who acts like a jealous husband who smothers the wife and will not allow her to act freely on her own volition. He seeks from people both attention and praise. He also tries to make a name for Himself. He will not share His position of honor with anyone else. He insists that He is the only authority and that His way is the only right way. Are these attitudes evidence of an unhealthy preoccupation with self that leads to narcissism (focusing on yourself so that you do not care about others)?[3] How can people worship such a God? How can they base their whole lives on such an appalling role model?[4] Because God claims to be the only God and that His way is the only way of salvation, He is charged with being a megalomaniac.

THE CLAIMS OF GOD

The Bible assumes the existence of God and declares that He is the one who has created the universe in which we live. Genesis 1:1 states, 'In the beginning God created the heavens and the earth'. God is the 'Creator' (Isa. 40:28;

---

2. Dawkins, *The God Delusion*, p. 276.
3. Paul Copan, *Is God a Moral Monster? Making Sense of the Old Testament God* (Ada: Baker Books, 2011), p. 27.
4. Dawkins, *The God Delusion*, p. 276.

Rom. 1:25; 1 Pet. 4:19). He not only created the world in which we live but He also created things in the world, such as animals and human beings (Gen. 1:21, 27). He created the heavens and the earth by the power of His spoken word (Gen. 1; Ps. 148:5) and will one day create a new heavens and earth (Isa. 65:17). As Creator, God has absolute authority over His creation and is working out His purposes within creation (Isa. 45:7), including His purposes for human beings. If you start a company, as the owner of that company you have control over the decisions that are made and the direction the company takes. It would be strange if someone else made all the daily decisions that must be made. Perhaps you might feel the necessity to get wisdom from others, but the buck stops with you as the owner. If you are working for a company, that company has the authority to require certain things of you as an employee. You may not always like some of those requirements, but many times your only option is to follow the directives of the company or quit your job. Or think of the artist who has control over his or her work of art. It is the artistic talent of the artist that is displayed in the work of art. If a potter is working with a piece of clay, the potter has authority over that clay to make whatever he or she wants to make. If a potter is working with a piece of clay and the clay does not turn out right, the potter is free to remake that clay into something else (Jer. 18:4). So, God has the same power over His creation, and it is futile for us to resist His will. More needs to be said, however, concerning God and His relationship to creation.

The character of the God of creation is so magnificent and glorious that He 'dwells in unapproachable light' (1 Tim. 6:16). He exists in a 'place' that is so far removed from human beings that we cannot and dare not look upon Him if the full manifestation of His glory and sovereignty are revealed. We are unable to stand before the radiance of His being. As mere creatures we would be consumed. When Moses asked to see God's glory as confirmation that God's presence would accompany the people in their journey to the land of Canaan (Exod. 33:18), God told Moses that He would make all His goodness pass before him. God's goodness here refers to all kinds of His wonderful benefits.[5] God will show Moses more than His glory by giving him a more profound understanding of His character. Yet, there is a limit to what God can show Moses because no human being can see the face of God and live (Exod. 33:20). Moses was only allowed to see the back of God. The terms 'face' and 'back' are human language that are used

---

5. Duane A. Garrett, *A Commentary on Exodus* (Grand Rapids: Kregel Publications, 2014), p. 638. Also, see Chapter 1 where the goodness of God is more fully discussed.

to describe God in ways we can understand (He is a spirit and does not literally have a face and a back). This incident describes the transcendence of God who is not only greater than human beings but is in a category all by Himself. As the Creator of the world, He exists outside of time and space and human beings are not able to stand before the full manifestation of His essence. When God's glory filled the tabernacle, Moses was not able to enter it (Exod. 40:34-35). A true understanding of the glory of God highlights the subordinate place of human beings before God and our frail condition. When Isaiah had his vision of the holiness and the glory of God, he fell on his face with a lament about the true character of humanity, 'I am a man of unclean lips, and dwell in the midst of a people of unclean lips; for my eyes have seen the King, the LORD of hosts!' (Isa. 6:5). Psalm 103:14 reminds us of the frailty of our condition when it states that God remembers that we are dust. Considering the greatness of God and our own limited knowledge of His works and His ways, we have no standing to challenge God's purposes (Rom. 9:19-20). Those who malign God's character and doubt His existence have no effect on God Himself and are like the person who stands in the face of the tornado and shakes his fist at it.

God is also eternally self-sufficient and satisfied. He needs nothing to complete His existence. And yet, out of the mere good pleasure of His will, He created this world, made creatures in His image, and revealed Himself to them. We would know nothing about God if not for His revelation in creation and in the Bible. What we know and see is only a glimpse of His glorious existence. God is not constrained by an inner deficiency or unhappiness to do anything He does not want to do. If God were unhappy, He would be deficient. He has been complete and fully satisfied from all eternity. He cannot be blamed for valuing what is of most value, that is, Himself. He needs no education, and no one can offer anything to Him that does not already come from Him (Rom. 11:34-36). He does not need our worship, but He is worthy of our worship. Human beings are so different from God because we have an immense void inside that craves satisfaction from powers and persons and pleasures outside of ourselves. We are born deficient, needy, and dissatisfied.[6] God is the only one who can fill this void in our lives.

God is not only the Creator of the universe, but He also sustains the universe. After affirming the deity of Christ, the author of Hebrews states that Christ upholds the universe by the word of His power (1:3). Other Scriptures speak of the deity of Christ (John 8:58-59;

---

6. John Piper, *The Pleasures of God* (Colorado Springs: Multnomah Books, 2000), p. 48-9.

Rom. 9:5; Col. 2:9) and His direct involvement in creating the world (John 1:3; Col. 1:16). Colossians 1:17 states that, 'he [Christ] is before all things, and in him all things hold together'. The fact that God not only created the universe but sustains it means that He is actively involved in the world. He is not a distant deity who is unconcerned about what happens in His creation. He did not create it, set it in motion, and then let it be governed only by the laws He established (a view called deism). Thus, He knows what is going on in His creation and, more importantly, He knows what is going on in your life. He continues to provide for His creation by making the sun to rise on the evil and the good and by sending rain on the just and the unjust (Matt. 5:45). He is a God you can call upon in time of need.

If God is the Creator of the heavens and the earth, then He is the only living and true God. No other gods exist besides Him (Isa. 45:5). He is 'the first and the last' (Isa. 44:6; 48:12), a phrase that refers to His unique sovereignty over everything that happens. As the first, He existed before the foundation of the world was laid, and, as the last, He will ensure that His will is accomplished for His creation. No one else can declare the end from the beginning because no one else can say, 'My counsel shall stand, and I will accomplish all my purpose' (Isa. 46:10). God is the sovereign Creator, so all creation is subject to

Him, including human beings. One day every knee will bow down to Him (Isa. 45:23). Even when someone does not believe in God, this act of unbelief adds to the glory of God. Psalm 76:10 states, 'Surely the wrath of man shall praise you'. When people are angry with God or shake their fists in His face, they serve the purposes of God. Human rebellion against God will come to nothing and may be used by God to display His power by destroying the wicked or by changing them to worship Him.

God does things 'for his name's sake'. It is amazing how many times this phrase is used in Scripture. It highlights why God is motivated to act in certain ways. God acts for the good of His people 'for his name's sake'. God acts to save His people (Ps. 25:11), which includes the forgiveness of their sins (Ps. 79:9), and He makes known His mighty power (Ps. 106:8). God brings His people out of trouble to preserve their lives (Ps. 143:11) so that He is the one we should appeal to when we are mistreated and abused (Ps. 109:21). God acts for the good of His people by leading them in paths of righteousness (Ps. 23:3). When Israel sinned and profaned God's name, He did not completely forsake them by destroying them; instead, He vindicated the holiness of His great name so that the nations would know that He was the LORD when He brought His people back from exile (Ezek. 36:22-23). God showed compassion toward His people by not dealing with them according to their evil ways so that they would know 'that I am the LORD' (Ezek. 20:44). God restrained His anger over His people's sin for His name's sake so that they might praise Him (Isa. 48:9). God is motivated to promote the honor of His name which led Him to treat His sinful people with great mercy. He could have justly destroyed them because they had profaned His name, but He desired for them to respect His name, so He kept His covenant promises and showed them great mercy. God delights to be known as merciful even in the face of the wickedness of people. This mercy was widespread as even outsiders came to Israel because they had heard of the great name of God and His mighty power to save (1 Kings 8:42). This lines up with God's promise to Abraham to be a blessing to the nations (Gen. 12:2-3), which is fulfilled in the Great Commission where the gospel is taken to all nations (Matt. 28:18-20).

The conclusion to be drawn from the Bible's presentation of God is that He is in a class all by Himself. There is none like Him in heaven and earth. Exodus 15:11 asks the rhetorical question:

> Who is like you, O LORD, among the gods?
> Who is like you, majestic in holiness,
> awesome in glorious deeds, doing wonders?

The expected answer is that no one is like the LORD among the gods. These questions occurred right after

God had delivered His people from Egypt by great demonstrations of His power in the plagues. The plagues clearly attacked the Egyptian gods (Exod. 12:12) and attacked Pharaoh, who was seen as a god by the Egyptians. God had also just delivered His people from the Egyptian army who drowned in the Red Sea. In poetic language the Song of victory described this: 'You stretched out your right hand; the earth swallowed them' (Exod. 15:12). The gods of Egypt were defeated by the LORD. God is also in a class by Himself when compared with human beings. We are weak, frail, and limited by space and time. God is strong and powerful and is not limited in any way. He is outside space and time. We are prone to evil and subject to death, but God is holy and pure and has the power to conquer death. We are finite, God is infinite. We cannot guarantee that any of our plans will succeed, but God is working out all things, including the wickedness of humanity, for His own glory and our good. God's plan will prevail, and the wondrous thing is that He invites unworthy sinners who repent of their wickedness and believe in Christ as the only one who can save them from their corruption to participate in His plan. It is a plan to redeem lost human beings and to restore creation. One day people from every nation, tribe, and language will sing the glory of His praises before His throne in celebration of His power to save and His grace toward the unworthy. You can become part of this victory celebration by confessing that Christ is Lord and that He is the only Savior who can deliver you from your corrupt nature.

IMPLICATIONS OF THE CLAIMS OF GOD

If a person takes an honest look at the claims of God as presented in the Bible, one will conclude that this God is very different from any of the other gods of the major or minor religions in the world. If God is in a class by Himself so that there is no other God or gods, or any other living creature like Him, then the charges brought against God at the beginning of this chapter are false charges. God is not a megalomaniac who suffers from false feelings of personal omnipotence and delusions of grandeur. Such people do not have a realistic view of themselves or their place in the world. If God has the power to create the universe and to carry out His plans for it, then He has a clear understanding of the world we live in and His relationship to the world. He does not think more highly of Himself than He ought to think and does not have delusional visions of grandeur. He can accomplish everything that He says He can accomplish. We recognize such competence on the human level. If Michael Jordan, during the height of his career, would claim that he should have the ball at the end of the game to take the last shot, no one would accuse him of thinking more highly of himself than he ought to think. His actions at the end of games matched his claims. Just google 'Michael Jordan Playoff Game Winners' and a video will show you all nine game-winning shots that he made *in the playoffs*. This is not boasting or false pride. Who else do you want to have the ball and take the last shot in a game other than Michael Jordan? He has a proven track record. God also has a proven track record. He can back up everything that He says and will one day demonstrate His power and glory to all creation. His purposes will be accomplished.

God is not 'jealous and proud of it' in the negative sense of that word. He does not react with the disordered emotion of monumental rage whenever His people flirt with a rival god. He is not a control freak who like a jealous husband smothers his wife and will not allow her to act freely on her own volition. These are false mischaracterizations of God's actions toward His people. When Adam rebelled against God, He instituted His plan to redeem humanity and restore creation. Part of that plan was to enter a covenant relationship with Abraham, and then later the descendants of Abraham at Mt. Sinai. God delivered His people from Egypt and brought them to Mt. Sinai to make them into a nation through a covenant. In that covenant God agreed to provide for His people and to be faithful to

His covenant promises, and the people agreed to obey the provisions of the covenant. Stipulations and sanctions were clearly laid out in the covenant that promised great blessing if the people would trust and obey God, and curses if the people disobeyed God. When Israel sought to worship other gods, they clearly violated the terms of the covenant and experienced God's judgment. God's covenant with Israel has similarities to a marriage covenant, where two people commit themselves exclusively to one another and pledge to be faithful to each other until death. This means that neither the husband nor the wife will seek to find their emotional or sexual needs fulfilled in any other person than the one to whom they are married. It is unfortunate that too many bad examples of jealous husbands exist who seek to control their wives in an inappropriate way. But there is a positive view of jealousy where both husband and wife have a zeal for what truly belongs to them because of their covenant commitments. A husband or wife should be angry when that which is truly theirs through a covenant agreement is given to someone else. It is appropriate to have a zeal for what is rightfully yours.

God demonstrates this proper zeal in His covenant relationships. In all God's covenant relationships, He has in view the good of those with whom He makes the covenant. Adam and Eve's life was a good life because God had provided everything they needed. They had freedom to eat from all the trees in the garden, except one. What a bounty God had provided for them. They had the ability to keep God's command not to eat from the tree of knowledge of good and evil, but they chose to disobey God's command and rebelled against the God who had given them so many good things. God had warned them that the consequences of disobedience would be death. Spiritual death is evident in Genesis 3 in Adam and Eve's reaction to God and to each other, and physical death follows in the later chapters of Genesis. Human beings became alienated from God and dominated by wickedness (Gen. 6:5). Even though God destroyed all living creatures except for Noah, his family, and the animals brought on the ark, He promised in His covenant with Noah that the cycles of the created order would continue so that His plan of redemption could be carried out in the Abrahamic, Mosaic, and Davidic covenants, culminating in the New Covenant.[7] Every time His people broke the covenant relationship, He was long-suffering and pursued His wayward people. We see this clearly in Hosea 1-3. God told Hosea to marry a woman who was sexually unfaithful. Although there is debate concerning when the sexual unfaithfulness occurred, it is possible that this

---

7. Abraham, Moses, and David are historic figures in Israel's history to whom God made major promises to redeem a people for Himself and we see those promises fulfilled in the New Covenant which is explained in the New Testament.

woman named Gomer had already been involved with several lovers. It is likely when Hosea married her that she was free of such lovers but instead of remaining faithful to her husband, she chased after other lovers. She sought her security from other men. By chapter 3 she was in a deplorable condition because her current lover was badly mistreating her. God told Hosea to go get Gomer, to purchase her freedom, and to bring her back to Himself. Hosea's marriage to Gomer is a picture of the relationship between God and Israel. God had entered a covenant with Israel that was to be an exclusive relationship. Israel was to worship only God, but she committed spiritual adultery by pursuing other gods. She sought her security and sustenance from the fertility god Baal (Hosea 2:7-8). God could have divorced His people and left them to the devastating results of judgment. But God pursued the very spouse who rejected Him and brought her back to Himself. He delivered her from bondage and restored her to the freedom of the covenant relationship. God demonstrated a zeal to pursue what was rightly His and, in the process, He showcased His commitment to His covenant promises. But Israel continued to pursue other gods. God was the jilted lover who pursued His bride, even though she rejected Him to go after other lovers.

The charge that God has an unhealthy preoccupation with Himself that leads to narcissism is a false charge which does not understand the nature of God, much less His character. God is not a deity who needs to have the praise of others to boost His ego or the companionship of others to keep Him from being lonely. The God of Scripture is presented as one God who exists in three persons, God the Father, God the Son, and God the Holy Spirit, who are one God and equal in power and glory. God is eternally self-sufficient and does not need anyone or anything outside of Himself. The persons of the Godhead are eternally in relationship with each other and so are not lonely, in need of human companionship. The nature and character of God is clear evidence that He does not care only about Himself; rather, He has provided everything good for His creation and for human beings who are made in His image. The problem is that many people live in such a way that ignores and rejects the very God who made them. Any person who rejects God, including atheists, is shaking their fists in the face of the God who created them while continuing to breathe the very air He has provided for them. Acts 17:28 reminds us that in God 'we live and move and have our being'. Our very existence depends on God moment by moment. God's goodness is constantly shown to those who do not believe in Him. He is the greatest source of blessing and help far beyond any earthly help we might receive, even from our parents. To show ingratitude to God is a great moral failure.

PROPER RESPONSE TO THE CLAIMS OF GOD

If God is who He claims to be, then the proper response is not to reject Him but to give Him the honor that He deserves. Scripture continually presents God as a God of glory. The Hebrew word for 'glory' (*kābēd*) has the basic meaning of 'heavy' but it is used in a figurative sense to refer to a person who is weighty in society, impressive, and thus should be respected. This word can refer to people who are noteworthy and impressive, but it especially refers to God. God is impressive because of the position He holds. As Creator of the universe God possesses greatness, power, victory, and glory because everything in the heavens and in the earth belongs to Him (1 Chron. 29:11). His glory is above the heavens (Ps. 113:4), but it is also demonstrated through creation (Ps. 19:1) and in His wondrous works to His people (Ps. 57:5, 11). The LORD of hosts is the King of glory (Ps. 24:7-10). The word 'hosts' refers to heavenly armies so that the LORD is a king with an army who fights for His people. God's victory over Pharaoh's chariot army is celebrated in Exodus 15 where God's glorious power is praised because He shattered the enemy (Exod. 15:6). When God comes in judgment people flee in terror before Him and from the splendor or glory of His majesty (Isa. 2:10).

The proper response that human beings should give to such a glorious God is worship because He is worthy of our adoration. The heavenly beings are commanded to worship God because He is worthy of glory, 'the glory due his name' (Ps. 29:1-2). All the earth is exhorted to worship God by singing the glory of His name because He is awesome in His deeds toward human beings (Ps. 66:1, 5). And of course, those who believe in Him as their Creator and Redeemer worship and bow down before Him (Ps. 95:6). God is worthy to be praised (Ps. 18:3). We should not view the commands to worship God as if He is craving 'for our worship like a vain woman who wants compliments'.[8] If God is the most glorious being in the universe, then a relationship with this God will be the most satisfying relationship we can have. Worship is adoration and we adore what delights us. We are commanded to delight ourselves in the LORD and He will give to us the desires of our hearts (Ps. 37:4). God is the source of complete and unending pleasure (Ps. 16:11).[9] We find our greatest delight in worshiping Him.

The emphasis on the glory of God continues into the New Testament but with an emphasis on the glory of Jesus Christ. In fact, the phrase 'to the praise of his glorious grace' is used of God the Father (Eph. 1:6) and the phrase 'to the praise of his glory' is used of

---

8. John Piper, *Desiring God* (Colorado Springs: Multnomah Publishers, 1996), p. 18, quoting C. S. Lewis.

9. Ibid., p. 19.

both God the Son (Eph. 1:12) and God the Holy Spirit (Eph. 1:14). All three persons of the Godhead are worthy of our praise. God is worthy of praise because He planned our salvation. The Holy Spirit is worthy of our praise because He sealed salvation to us. And Jesus Christ is worthy of praise because He carried out the plan of salvation by coming to the earth to pay the penalty for our wickedness. Because Christ is the one who accomplished our salvation, there is an emphasis on His glory alongside the glory of the Father (Gal. 1:5; Rev. 1:6). Jesus Christ is the Word of God who became flesh and dwelt among His people. The verb that is used in John 1:14 for 'dwelt' is a verb that is used in reference to the tabernacle. In the Old Testament, the tabernacle, and then later the temple, was the special place of God's presence where the glory of God manifested itself. When the tabernacle was first built and was ready to be used as a place of worship and sacrifice, the glory of God so filled it that Moses was not able to enter (Exod. 40:35). The same thing happened at the dedication of the temple under Solomon. The priests could not minister in the temple because the cloud of the glory of God filled it (1 Kings 8:10-11). This glory was visible to the people in the pillar of cloud by day and the pillar of fire by night which led the people out of Egypt (Exod. 13:21) and in the wilderness after they left Mt. Sinai (Num. 10:33-34).

The apostle John affirms that the disciples also saw the glory of God in Jesus (John 1:14). He fulfills what the tabernacle/temple stood for. He is Immanuel, God with us, the one who demonstrates the glory of God in His life and ministry. Jesus Christ gave His life for my salvation by dying on the cross for my sin, by being resurrected from the dead, and by ascending into heaven so that He now sits as king over this world directing all things for the good of His people. The proper response is for us to give everything we have to this glorious and wondrous God. No matter what we do in life we should do it to the glory of Christ (1 Cor. 10:31). We should be willing to offer our bodies as living sacrifices to the service of our king (Rom. 12:1). Jesus Christ is worth living for and He is also worth dying for. We have the privilege of living for Him in this life and rejoicing in His glory for all eternity.

SUMMARY OF MAIN POINTS

- God as the Creator of the world has complete authority over His creation, including the lives of human beings.

- A proper view of the exalted character of God as transcendent and self-sufficient helps us understand how frail we are as human beings, but it also gives us confidence that God has the power to accomplish His purposes of salvation for us and His creation.

- God is not a megalomaniac because He is able to back up all the claims that He makes.

- God is not a jealous God in the negative sense of the word, but He demonstrates a zeal for His people by pursuing them even when they disobey Him.

- The proper response to the glory of God is to give Him the honor He deserves by worshiping Him in whom we find our greatest delight.

- The glory of God manifested to God's people in the pillar of cloud and fire and in the tabernacle is also manifested in Jesus Christ, God with us, who is worthy of our worship and complete dedication.

7

Implications of Living
Life Without God

IS RELIGION THE MAJOR PROBLEM WE FACE?

This book has sought to address some of the misconceptions that people have about God, especially the God of the Old Testament. These misconceptions have been at the forefront of many of the New Atheists' writings against God and the morality of the Bible. Not only have we tried to answer these objections through a better understanding of what the Bible teaches, but we have also tried to show some of the implications for morality, and for life itself, when God is removed from the discussion. This chapter will discuss whether Christianity, or religion in general, is a major contributor to the violence and hatred we experience in the world and whether the solution is to abolish Christianity. The conclusion will be that the worldview of atheism has its own serious moral problems and it is anti-theism (any view that denies God) rather than the 'moral monster' of biblical theism that invites societal violence.

DAWKINS' VIEW OF RELIGION

Dawkins places a lot of blame on religion in general, including Christianity, for the problems we face in the world. His view of religion is summed up in the following statement:

> Though the details differ across the world, no known culture lacks some version of the time-consuming, wealth-consuming, hostility provoking rituals, the anti-factual, counter-productive fantasies of religion.[1]

Although he does not believe that religious people are mad, in the sense of being silly or stupid, he does believe religious *beliefs* are silly and stupid. Theologians have nothing worthwhile to say. Religion endangers the lives of other people because of its narrow views. The evidence is the many examples of people who have been tortured or killed because of their beliefs. Dawkins recognizes that religion is a universal phenomenon found in every culture, and he seeks to explain it within a Darwinian framework. He does not believe that religion has a survival value of its own because it is a by-product of something

---

1. Richard Dawkins, *The God Delusion* (New York: Mariner Books, 2008), p. 194.

else. Asking why people die for such beliefs is asking the wrong question. Religious behavior may be a misfiring, an unfortunate by-product of an underlying psychological propensity which in other circumstances is, or once was, useful. So, what is the primitively advantageous trait that sometimes misfires to generate religion?[2]

One of Dawkins' hypotheses concerns children. For a child's brain to operate with the rule of thumb that they must believe, without question, whatever their grown-ups tell them has a selective advantage. Trust your elders is a generally valid rule for a child, but this can go wrong because they are vulnerable to believing anything they are told, such as the idea that religion is good for them. Thus, their minds become infected with the virus of religion. When they grow up and become parents, they also pass on the same nonsense. Although religion has some value in bringing consolation and comfort, it is no different than when children find value in an imaginary friend. In the same way, God is an imaginary being who seems real and gives comfort and advice. Dawkins defines religious faith as belief without evidence. Thus, the ideas of one religion are not any better than the ideas of any other religion in an absolute sense.[3] However, he concludes that we can give up belief in God and the supernatural while not losing

2.   Ibid., pp. 80, 113, 192-3, 200, 202.
3.   Ibid., p. 232.

touch with a treasured heritage found in the Bible on a literary level and experienced in marriages and funerals.[4]

ALL RELIGIONS ARE NOT THE SAME

If someone tries to argue that religion is the major cause behind the problems we face in the world, one expects a discussion of the significant differences between the various religions of the world. Even if one rejects all religions, all religions are not the same; in fact, religions make exclusive claims which are different. Many in our culture reject exclusive claims outright in an attempt not to be judgmental or offensive because they believe that any exclusive view is wrong. This is not a reasonable position because if Christians are right about Jesus being God, then Muslims and Jews are wrong about God. If Muslims and Jews are right about Jesus not being God, then Christians are wrong about God.[5] Beliefs make a difference. Of course, atheists see themselves above the fray because they reject all religious claims. Science is the way to truth over against religious claims. This is a false dichotomy. Atheistic science (Darwinian evolution) based on a naturalistic, material view of the world can at most explain what exists; it cannot legislate what should be morally.[6]

---

4. Ibid., p. 387.

5. Mark Clark, *The Problem of God: Answering a Skeptic's Challenges to Christianity* (Grand Rapids: Zondervan, 2017), p. 213.

6. Ransom Poythress, *Has Science Made God Unnecessary?* (Ross-shire: Christian Focus Publications, 2022), pp. 53-78.

Even if atheists have no philosophical basis for morality, atheists can live in a 'moral' way. In fact, it is not unusual for people to live next to a Muslim, Jewish, or atheist neighbor and get along very well. It is also possible that such a neighbor could be rude and difficult. Bad apples exist in every group. There are certainly Christians who are hypocrites. Every group has its own issues. For example, many would point out that the Jewish people exterminated the Canaanites, Christians participated in the Crusades, Muslims committed atrocities against Christians in Iraq and Syria, and totalitarian regimes which rejected God put to death millions of people.

And yet, to place all these groups on the same level and argue that what they believe has made no difference in history is a grave misunderstanding. The Jewish extermination of the Canaanites was limited to a particular time and was not the normal practice of Israel who rarely engaged in offensive warfare. For many periods of Jewish history, they have been the oppressed who have been targeted for extermination (the Holocaust). The several Crusades of Christians (from a.d. 1095 to a.d. 1187) were a response to centuries of Muslim aggression against Christianized lands and the conquest of Jerusalem.[7] Not everything that

---

7.   Rebecca McLaughlin, *Confronting Christianity: 12 Hard Questions for the World's Largest Religion* (Wheaton: Crossway, 2019), p. 77.

'Christians' did during the Crusades can be justified, but the initial response was a defensive reaction against aggression to protect citizens and to reclaim lands overrun by Muslims. If one compares Scripture with the Quran, the differences are startling. The founder of Christianity, Jesus Christ, did not lead an army but laid down His life as a sacrifice for sin to offer forgiveness to those who have offended God and are considered His enemies. The founder of Islam, Muhammad, engaged in over sixty military campaigns to conquer and force Islam on other countries. Christianity spreads by preaching the gospel of the good news of forgiveness of sin through faith in Jesus Christ and Islam spreads by military conquest. The Quran contains many harsh militaristic passages that seek to subject all infidels to conversion to Islam or they will face the consequences of unbelief. Historically, Islamic leaders have sought to establish a theocratic state where Shariah law rules both the religious community and the political realm. Anyone who does not comply with Shariah law can be persecuted and even executed. Conservative forms of Islam that adhere closely to the teachings of the Quran and Muhammad do not treat women very well and limit the freedom people have to think and live the way they want. Many times, liberals in the West downplay this aspect of Islam, so much so that the myth of Muslim toleration is a modern creation of the West.[8] Who can forget the Islamic woman with a sign around her neck proclaiming, 'Behead those who think that Islam is a violent religion'.[9] The point is not that all Muslims who live in the West are violent, but you cannot lump all religions together and condemn them all with one stroke because religions are different in what they believe which affects how their adherents live.

THE POSITIVE BENEFITS OF CHRISTIANITY

Christianity and true followers of Jesus Christ have had a profound positive effect in history. To say that all religions are equally true is to lose an important perspective on history.[10] Christians have been at the forefront of establishing hospitals, the development of medicine, social reforms related to children and work, educational reforms to make education available to all, resisting tyrannical government rulers who restrict basic human freedoms, and seeking reconciliation after war and genocide.[11] It is irresponsible to argue that religion poisons everything and is a virus

8. Paul Copan, *Is God a Moral Monster? Making Sense of the Old Testament God* (Ada: Baker, 2011), p. 204.

9. David Robertson, *The Dawkins Letters: Challenging Atheist Views* (Ross-shire: Christian Focus Publications, 2013, rev. ed.), p. 38.

10. McLaughlin, *Confronting Christianity*, p. 54.

11. For examples of this kind of activity see William Edgar, *Does Christianity Really Work?* (Ross-shire: Christian Focus Publications, 2016).

of the mind that must be eradicated. Studies show that specific biblical commands have many benefits. Although this does not prove that religion or these commands are true, the evidence is contrary to the idea that religion is bad for people. The 'seven counterintuitive biblical commands' that are beneficial include: it is more blessed to give than to receive, the love of money disappoints, work is meaningful when understood as a calling, people can be content in all circumstances, gratitude is good for us, self-control and perseverance help people thrive, and we need something larger than ourselves (such as God). These benefits are particularly evident in one who commits himself or herself to faith in Jesus Christ. Other groups, whether religious or not, can benefit from these principles. It is not a surprise that Dawkins would argue for the benefit of living in an altruistic way toward others (living in a way that shows care and concern for other people).[12] But even he recognizes that it is difficult to establish this way of life based on Darwinian evolution when he states that he is a passionate Darwinian when it comes to science and 'a passionate anti-Darwinian when it comes to politics and how we should conduct human affairs'.[13] His fallback is that evolution has given us big enough brains that we

---

12. Dawkins, *Delusion*, pp. 247-53.
13. Richard Dawkins, *A Devil's Chaplain: Reflections on Hope, Lies, Science, and Love* (Mariner, 2004), pp. 10-11.

are able to deplore certain moral implications of evolution and fight against them. This is a huge concession because within a materialistic worldview there is no reason to think that the moral implications of evolution are to be rejected.[14]

THE PROPER VIEW OF THE ROLE OF FAITH

Another misunderstanding of religion, particularly Christianity, is the role of faith. Dawkins defines faith as belief without evidence. He concludes that faith is an evil because it requires no justification and brooks no argument. It is a kind of mental illness. Science is different because it deals with evidence and is the way to truth over against the claims of religion. In fact, science should replace the role of religion because it can explain, exhort, console, and inspire better than religion.[15] Several things are wrong with this very simplistic view of the differences between faith and science. Dawkins does not present any reasons for his view that Christian faith is blind trust or belief without evidence. He does not quote any major Christian theologians who hold this view because they do not exist. This is not a view of faith held by Christians. It is his own definition constructed to further his own agenda. It allows him to put faith in God in the same category as belief in the Tooth Fairy or Santa Claus which are mere childish

---

14. McLaughlin, *Confronting Christianity*, p. 121.
15. Dawkins, *Delusion*, pp. 232, 346, and 389.

beliefs. It is an easy straw man for Dawkins to knock down. His view that faith is blind trust does not stand up to serious investigation and is an excellent example of Dawkins himself advocating a false belief tenaciously held and defended in the absence of evidence.[16]

THE PROPER VIEW OF THE ROLE OF SCIENCE

Dawkins' view of the role of science falls short of how science really operates. He views Darwinian evolution driven by natural selection as a worldview that can explain everything in the universe. But science is limited in what it can do. The natural sciences rely on observation and experiment in investigating the world. This limits science to solving problems that can be investigated through observation and the testing of hypotheses. Christianity has no issues with this method of science. In fact, Christians were at the forefront of the development of science.[17] A theological foundation exists for the laws of science.[18] Christians have issues with

---

16. Alister E. McGrath, *Dawkins' God: From the Selfish Gene to the God Delusion*, 2nd ed. (Hoboken: John Wiley & Sons, Ltd., 2015), pp. 60-3, 69. This is a very helpful book for understanding Dawkins' development even if it is a little too comfortable with evolution.

17. R. Hooykaas, *Religion and the Rise of Modern Science* (Grand Rapids: Eerdmans, 1972); McLaughlin, *Confronting Christianity*, p. 111.

18. Poythress, *Has Science Made God Unnecessary?*, pp. 82-108; James N. Anderson, 'The Laws of Nature and Nature's God: The Theological Foundations of Modern Science', *Reformed Faith & Practice*, 4.1 (May 2019), pp. 4-16 (https://journal.rts.edu/article/

some of the theories of science. Science is not equipped to solve all our problems or to speculate on questions that are beyond its limits, such as the origin of the world or what is morally good.[19] The so-called war between Christianity and science is greatly overblown.[20]

In scientific investigation of the world, theories are believed to be accurate until the evidence shows that a different explanation works better. In fact, what scientists believe today about many things is different from what scientists have believed in the past. It is impossible to take an absolute position on the question of whether any given theory is right. As one author notes, history makes fools of those who argue that every aspect of the current theoretical situation is true for all time.[21] Many theories of science are provisional, the best account of the experimental observations available. Although Dawkins acknowledges the possibility that new facts may emerge that would cause our successors to reject or significantly modify Darwin's views,[22] he treats Darwinian evolution

---

the-laws-of-nature-and-of-natures-god-the-theological-foundations-of-modern-science/).

19. Michael J. Kruger, *Surviving Religion 101: Letters to a Christian Student on Keeping the Faith in College* (Wheaton: Crossway, 2021), p. 127; McGrath, *Dawkins' God*, p. 81.

20. Poythress, *Has Science Made God Unnecessary?*, pp. 20-22; Kruger, *Surviving Religion 101*, p. 127.

21. McGrath, *Dawkins' God*, p. 79.

22. Dawkins, *A Devil's Chaplain*, p. 81.

not as a scientific theory but as an absolute worldview that explains every aspect of human existence and behavior.

DARWINIAN EVOLUTION AS A WORLDVIEW

Darwinian evolution as a worldview cannot explain everything in life. If the natural sciences proceed by inference from observational data, how can Dawkins be so sure that his current beliefs are true when history shows a persistent pattern of abandoning scientific theories as better approaches emerge?[23] In addition, how can Dawkins be so sure about atheism? Rather, inductive reasoning based on observation must presuppose the uniformity of nature. An experiment done today under certain conditions will have the same result today, tomorrow, or next year if conducted under the same conditions. The scientific method cannot prove the uniformity of nature based on inductive reasoning. In other words, the scientific method depends on a form of reasoning that the scientific method itself cannot prove but assumes to be true. Is this not a leap of faith or blind trust?[24] Science itself developed in the context of a theistic worldview that supplied a rationale for the uniformity of nature based on God as the Creator and sustainer of the universe, a transcendent

23. McGrath, *Dawkins' God*, p. 87.
24. Anderson, 'Laws of Nature and Nature's God', pp. 11-12.

omniscient being.[25] Modern science also could not exist without mathematics. The laws of nature are formulated in mathematical terms. Numbers are real but they are not material, visible things. Mathematics trades in abstract, timeless, necessary truths, rather than contingent facts about the material world. They are not known empirically by observation but through self-evident, immediate apprehension (*a priori* intuition) and deduction. Such order cannot be explained by modern science, but it makes perfect sense in a Christian worldview.[26] Dawkins' certainty about atheism and Darwinian evolution is itself based on assumptions which he cannot prove. He may believe that Darwinism is right, but he does not know that this is so. As McGrath states:

> The grounds of Dawkins' atheism lies elsewhere than his science ... Dawkins uses an inductive approach to defend a Darwinian world view – yet then extracts from this worldview a set of premises from which secure conclusions may be deduced ... Having inferred that Darwinism is the best explanation of observation, Dawkins proceeds to transmute a provisional scientific theory into a totalizing ideological worldview. Atheism is thus presented as the logical conclusion of a series of axiomatic premises ...[27]

---

25. Poythress, *Has Science Made God Unnecessary?* pp. 91-108.
26. Anderson, 'Laws of Nature and Nature's God', pp. 14-15.
27. McGrath, *Dawkins' God*, pp. 70-1.

In other words, Dawkins' belief in atheism does not arise from his scientific worldview. His conclusions do not follow from the starting point of his argument. You cannot begin with an inductive approach (an approach that begins with the evidence of the world in which we live) and come up with universal principles. It is impossible to argue from observed facts to moral values as this has serious implications for understanding Darwinian evolution as a worldview.

THE PROBLEM OF MORALITY

If religion, including Christianity, is not good for people, what is good for people? What kind of morality might we expect if one adheres to Darwinian evolution as a worldview? Dawkins' view of religion is that it evolved not because it was true, but because it helped the species to survive. It developed as a psychological coping mechanism to explain what people were not able to explain with the result that it brought great comfort to people. In other words, even though religion is false and endangers the lives of people because its views are silly and stupid, it evolved because it helped the species survive. This confirms that natural selection is not concerned about what is true or false but is only concerned about survivability. Thus, it is impossible to base any kind of universal moral system on natural selection because naturalistic evolution is blind. It has no consciousness, or intelligence or knowledge.[28] Anything that evolves from natural selection would partake of the same characteristics. Thus, there is no reason to think that these human faculties within a Darwinian worldview would lead us toward moral truth and away from falsehood. To argue otherwise is to make unwarranted assumptions.[29]

In a Darwinian worldview, human beings are not special because they are human but should be considered no different with respect to moral status than any other species. If there is no morally relevant distinction between species, how do we make decisions when we must distinguish between species? The basic principle is that based on evolution you cannot grant unique special rights to human beings (Homo sapiens) over against other species.[30] Only on a Christian worldview are human beings morally distinct from animals. Human beings have moral obligations which include the moral obligation to look after the welfare of animals (Prov. 12:10; Jonah 4:11; Exod. 23:12; Deut. 22:6-7).

The implications for treating human beings on the same level as other species are tragic because no longer

---

28. Anderson, 'Laws of Nature and Nature's God', p. 13.
29. Ibid., p. 8.
30. Ibid., pp. 336, 339.

is human life sacred. The overwhelming majority of Christians condemned Paul Hill's murder of the abortion doctor,[31] while at the same time also condemning the taking of human life in the womb. What separates human fetuses from the fetuses of chimpanzees is that human beings are made in the image of God (Gen. 1:26-28). What separates human suffering from the suffering of animals is the image of God. A human being has dignity because each human being reflects the image of God. Dawkins believes that belief in God can be abandoned while not losing touch with a treasured heritage found in the Bible that people experience in marriages and funerals without having to believe in the supernatural.[32] Such a view might work in Western societies that still have a historical relationship to Judeo-Christian principles, but in other societies the results can be catastrophic. Any society that loses the special character of human beings made in the image of God is in danger of treating its subjects as animals. If God is removed from the picture, there are no boundaries to which people will go to hurt each other. It should not be a surprise that totalitarian governments over the centuries have slaughtered billions of people. Dawkins is concerned that parents are not

---

31. https://www.baptistpress.com/resource-library/news/paul-hill-executed-leaders-say-he-has-hurt-the-pro-life-cause/

32. Ibid., p. 387.

allowed to impose their beliefs on their children, but it is totalitarian regimes like the Soviet Union and other atheistic governments that have imposed their beliefs on those that they govern.[33] Even though emancipation from religion was supposed to bring about utopia on earth, when God died in the nineteenth century, the twentieth century became bloodier than any previous century.

AN ANALYSIS OF SOCIETY WITHOUT GOD

The real problem we face is not religion but living life without God. In 1 and 2 Timothy, Paul writes to his younger colleague Timothy as he draws near to the end of his life. Paul's goal from his first letter was to help Timothy 'know how one ought to behave in the household of God, which is the church of the living God, a pillar and buttress of the truth' (1 Tim. 3:15). In the second letter Paul encourages Timothy not to be ashamed of the gospel and to be faithful to pass on the truth of God's Word. The necessity of vigilance and perseverance is because of what Timothy may face in the days ahead. Paul gives a sobering analysis of the times that lie ahead (2 Tim. 3:1-9). He uses the term 'last days' which in the New Testament refers to the time-period between the first and second coming of Christ. He describes these times as 'times of difficulty'. The word 'difficulty' stresses violence. It is used of the violence

---

33. McGrath, *Dawkins' God*, p. 66.

of the two demon-possessed men in Matthew 8:28. They were so violent that no one could pass by them. Paul uses 18 or 19 descriptive words to describe the violence.[34] What is the cause of the violence? The character of the people described is what makes the times so violent. A closer look at the list that describes their character is revealing.

A MISGUIDED LOVE

The structure of 2 Timothy 3:2-4 emphasizes the word 'love' (*philos*), but it is love directed toward the wrong things. At the very beginning of the list people are described as 'lovers of self' and 'lovers of money'. When self becomes the focus of life every other relationship becomes distorted because no longer are you concerned about others, but you are only concerned about yourself. Life is viewed through the lens of what is in it for me, what works best for me. Money is the way in which all your desires can be fulfilled so a pursuit of money naturally follows. Since we never have enough, the love of money can become an all-consuming pursuit to the neglect of other important relationships and activities. In the middle of the list toward the end of verse 3 is the phrase 'not loving good'. The word 'good' can have in view what is beneficial for others, so this phrase emphasizes that such

---

34. Robert W. Yarbrough, *The Letters to Timothy and Titus* (Grand Rapids: Eerdmans, 2018), pp. 404, 410.

people have no interest in the common good and what makes for a peaceful existence with others. At the end of the list in verse 4 is the phrase 'lovers of pleasure rather than lovers of God'. Self-gratification takes center stage in a person's life and becomes the most important thing in life. Instead of life revolving around God as the center, the satisfaction of my desires becomes the center of life. Money and pleasure become idols that dominate a person's life. The main characteristic of the people described in this list is a distorted view of love. They do not know who to love, what to love, or how to love because they have rejected God, who is love (1 John 4:16).

The rest of the characteristics of the list follow when a large proportion of people in a society become individual self-seekers of their own pleasure because their concept of love is distorted. If a person is consumed with self-love, then pride, arrogance, and abuse will follow. People boast about themselves and look down on others with contempt. Such attitudes and behavior lead to the breakdown of relationships, even family relationships. A general disrespect of authority develops, which starts in the home with disobedience to parents. Parents might be at fault if they are consumed with their own self-interests but also many times sons and daughters do not honor their parents because they are ungrateful. They do not appreciate the love and sacrifice that their parents make for them because they are consumed by self. In verse 3 a word is used that can mean 'heartless' or 'without natural affection'. We generally expect natural affection to develop in the family, but when love is misguided toward the wrong things, an atmosphere for love to grow and flourish is not promoted. Instead, toxic relationships develop where people become irreconcilable and are not willing to work toward forgiveness and reconciliation. A loss of self-control that manifests itself in both words and actions takes over. It becomes easy to slanderously speak evil of others, which has become rampant in a cancel culture where people hide behind anonymity to spew their hateful rhetoric. People become 'brutal' toward each other, a word that can also mean 'savage' which would emphasize that we treat each other more like animals than humans. Too many horrific instances of child abuse occur that exemplify the brutality in our culture today. The sad thing is that many who act this way appear on the outside to be outstanding members of society who have prestigious positions but act in reckless ways.

THE BASIC NATURE OF HUMAN BEINGS

It will be hard for many of us to recognize ourselves in these characteristics, but if we are honest with ourselves, everyone struggles with these negative character traits. The reason is that all of us have been deeply affected by a human nature that is flawed by wickedness. Part of the reason we do not recognize ourselves in these characteristics is because we have fooled ourselves to think that we are pretty good people. We have believed the lie of our culture that people are in essence good. The cultural concept of evil in the Western world has become distorted. We either have no concept of sin, or we have trivialized sin by limiting it to the dessert menu (sinful chocolate cake) or by associating it with things which people have no control over (being born a certain color with certain privileges). We have become like the false teachers of Paul's own day who were 'opposed to the truth'. We have been deceived by outward appearances because people look respectable, sound reasonable, and give a good impression. But apart from the truth of God we are easily led astray by various passions, deceived concerning what is good and true, and corrupted in our minds so that we are never able to come to the knowledge of the truth.

The Western world has lived a long time on the remnants of a Judeo-Christian view of life. Even when God has been relegated to the sidelines, the vestiges of that worldview can be seen in the way people have treated each other because of a commitment to truth and a certain form of morality. More and more the implications for living life without God have become apparent in our culture. Without God universal truth does not exist. We are left on our own in a post-modern world where what is true for me is not necessarily true for you. We are caught in a battle for whose individual truth will win the day. In such a situation there is no longer a standard to judge what people think or do. Love becomes an individual expression of what is good for me even if it harms you. Morality becomes what I think is good for me whether it is good for anyone else. In our culture today we have many people who are committed to this way of thinking so that it looks like this view is dominant. Political correctness has become the measure by which people are destroyed socially, economically, and personally. People can no longer discuss different opinions because some opinions have been declared out of bounds. There are few reasoned arguments today in social media and so we are left with people screaming at each other as they try to advance their views.

We have acknowledged in this book that not everyone who denies the existence of God is going to live a raunchy life of immorality, but without God no consistent basis for morality exists. As noted earlier, even Richard Dawkins has stated that he does not want to be governed by the moral implications of Darwinian evolution. He describes himself as a passionate Darwinian when it comes to science and a passionate anti-Darwinian when it comes to politics and how we should conduct human affairs. The reason we can reject the moral implications of Darwinian evolution is because our brains have evolved to the size where it can understand the moral implications of evolution and of fighting against them.[35] In other words, we need evolution to explain how we got here as human beings without God, but the very process of evolution would lead to a life of meaninglessness with no moral compass, so we need to elevate the human species to a place where we are able to reject the implications of the very process that explains our existence. An evolutionary process grounded in the view that only matter exists cannot at the end of the day reject the implications of that process just because we are appalled at the moral implications. This assumes a standard of morality by which to judge the implications of evolution, but a materialistic process cannot lead to a human species that is concerned with spiritual or moral matters. No other product of evolution in the animal world has these concerns. Why should human beings? Having put all your emphasis on a process that is materialistic, you cannot bring a standard of morality in the back door.

---

35. Dawkins, *A Devil's Chaplain*, pp. 10-11 and *The Selfish Gene* (Oxford: Oxford University Press, 2006), p. 200.

THE NECESSITY OF GOD

If there is no moral authority that governs human behavior, there is no reason for us to treat each other any different than we treat our animals. We can be thankful that not everyone who does not believe in God is consistent in the way they live their lives. Even atheists reflect the image of their Creator when they argue for living in ways that would benefit others. Without God there is no true understanding of love, no universal truth, and no universal standard of morality. If one adds to this mix that humans are flawed because they generally act in their own self-interest, one is left with a deadly formula of human beings promoting their own agendas over against the good of others. In Christian terms, this is called sin and it is not something our current culture even recognizes. The denial of sin, however, is catastrophic for how people treat each other and explains a lot that is going on in the Western world. Without a concept of sin, we are not able to hold people responsible for their actions. In 1973 a psychiatrist by the name of Karl Menninger wrote a book entitled, *Whatever Became of Sin?* In that book he lamented the fact that the word 'sin' has disappeared from our vocabulary. What used to be sinful is now a symptom of a disease. The concept of sin has been replaced by legal, medical, or scientific terms. Dr. Menninger laments the disappearance of the concept of sin because without it there is no concept of responsibility. A 'no fault' theology develops where no one is really to blame for what they have done.[36] For example, many parents no longer hold their children responsible for their actions. They want to make their children happy, so they give to them unearned praise, relinquish authority to them, and protect them from any criticism. Obedience is no longer valued.[37] Such overindulgence leads to narcissism in children where they believe the world revolves around them. Another example of this type of thinking is the way society seeks to help the poor. Instead of helping people to develop a work ethic, we give handouts, which in the long run devastate their self-worth and hinder their ability to provide for themselves.[38] We see criminals as victims, and let many dangerous people go free without holding them responsible for their actions.[39] Also, people begin to believe that if we just show people compassion and

---

36. Karl Menninger, *Whatever Became of Sin?* (New York: Bantam Books, 1978 reprint).

37. Jean Twenge and Keith Campbell, 'Parenting: Raising Royalty', in *The Narcissism Epidemic: Living in the Age of Entitlement* (New York: Free Press, 2009), pp. 73-89.

38. Marvin Olasky, *The Tragedy of American Compassion* (Wheaton: Crossway, 2008), especially Chapter 3.

39. For example, 'New Manhattan District Attorney Announces Changes to Unleash Anarchy' (https://townhall.com/tipsheet/spencerbrown/2022/01/05/new-manhattan-district-attorney-announces-changes-to-benefit-criminals-n2601445)

reassure them that we mean them no harm, they will respond in kind. But evil people do not live that way. A tragic case is a couple who believed evil was a made-up concept. They biked all over the world to demonstrate this belief. Sadly, as they rode through Tajikistan which borders Afghanistan, they were attacked and killed by men who pledged allegiance to ISIS.[40]

When the power of government is added to these views, governments easily become instruments of oppression that deny the basic freedom of human beings. Governments in history that have been responsible for the most deaths are governments where the leaders have rejected God, particularly communistic and totalitarian governments. Sixty-one million were killed in the former Soviet Union. Thirty-five million lost their lives in the People's Republic of China. Smaller communist states have also slaughtered many (North Korea and Cambodia, for example). The sheer numbers killed by governments through deadly purges, lethal prison camps, murderous forced labor, and outright mass murder is almost impossible to digest. Before concluding that religion is the problem, we must acknowledge that an anti-religious ideology has led governments to commit atrocious acts.[41]

---

40. https://www.dailywire.com/news/american-couple-believing-evil-make-believe-hank-berrien
41. McLaughlin, *Confronting Christianity*, pp. 81-2.

A source of universal truth must exist or else we have no hope of enforcing a standard of morality. A book called the Bible gives us the basis for a universal standard of morality. It sets forth a God who is above the created world but also very involved in the world. He is all-powerful and sovereign, knows all things, and is also very gracious and full of mercy. The evidence of His existence is embedded in the order of nature. Although some claim not to see any evidence for His existence, the reality is that science itself could not operate without the stability in creation and the regularity of the way nature works. The mathematical precision of the world in which we live is stunning and is not possible without an infinite mind behind it. Time and chance do not produce a world that operates with consistent rules (like gravity), and evolution cannot produce a morality that is universal and applies to everyone.

God is a gracious God who has our best interests in view. He has given us His Word so that we can live a blessed and fulfilling life. The basis of such a life is found in the Bible.[42] After Paul describes what happens to a society that operates on a misguided view of love (2 Tim. 3:1-9), he exhorts Timothy to be different. Instead of getting swept up in the direction that everyone else in society is going, Timothy is to base his life on the truth of the

---

42. Timothy Paul Jones, *Why Should I Trust the Bible?* (Ross-shire: Christian Focus Publications, 2019).

Word of God. Even though evil people and imposters will grow worse because they are deceived about life, Timothy is to continue to stay the course through a commitment to the Scriptures which are able to make him wise for salvation through faith in Christ (2 Tim. 3:15). Such a life will lead to persecution (3:12), but it is a life based on the sure foundation of what God has spoken. Scripture itself teaches that its source is God Himself (3:16), and therefore it is profitable for teaching us how we are to live and what we are to believe. Negatively, Scripture reproves and corrects us when what we think or do goes against what God has revealed in His Word. God does not give us negative commands because He enjoys being strict and confining the way we live, but because as our Creator He knows what kind of life will lead to fulfillment and satisfaction. A locomotive can pull its heavy load when it sits on a set of railroad tracks made for it. So, we can live a fulfilling life as we live in the way we have been created to live. Although our own wickedness and the prospect of death seem to be major obstacles for us to live a full and satisfying life, the death of Jesus on the cross, followed by His resurrection, is God's victorious response to the prospect of the destructive power of sin and death. Jesus paid the penalty for sin by taking on Himself the punishment for our wickedness, and legally crediting to our account His righteousness. When God looks at us through Christ, He does not see our sin but Christ's righteousness. Christ's resurrection from the dead guarantees that we will be victorious over death. One day we will be resurrected from the dead and enjoy eternal life with God our Father and Jesus our Savior in a new heavens and new earth. This hope can be yours if you trust in Jesus for your salvation. He has the power to transform your life now and for all eternity.

SUMMARY OF MAIN POINTS

- Many atheists argue that religion is the cause of the problems in the world today because they believe it contributes to the violence and hatred we see in the world.

- It is wrong to lump all religions together because all religions do not teach the same things and some religions, like Christianity, have contributed to the benefit and welfare of people.

- Dawkins' definition of religious faith as blind trust that is belief without evidence does not stand up to serious investigation and is an example of Dawkins himself advocating a false belief in the absence of evidence.

- Science is limited in the questions it can answer and Darwinian evolution isn't a worldview that explains everything; it is very limited in what it can explain.

- The scientific method assumes the regularity of the laws of nature and their mathematical formulations because it is impossible to start with the premise of naturalistic materialism and logically conclude that the world is an ordered world; in other words, science assumes certain things that it cannot prove.

- It is impossible to base a universal moral system on evolution by natural selection because it is not concerned about what is true or false and it does not operate with consciousness or intelligence.

- When a society does not believe in God, people operate with a misguided love that focuses on themselves leading to a breakdown of basic human relationships and fostering violence toward others (1 Tim. 3:1-11).

- We must be honest with ourselves and recognize that human nature is flawed because wickedness is deeply engrained within us and without such a recognition, we are unable to hold people responsible for their actions and call them to self-sacrifice for others.

- Totalitarian governments who do not believe in God have been the most oppressive regimes, denying people basic freedoms and killing more people than any other human organization.

- The God revealed in the Bible is the Creator of the world and is the source of universal truth, a universal standard of morality, the order in nature, the regularity of the laws of nature, and the mathematical precision of the world.

- The God of the Bible is not a capricious, moral monster but is a God who loves and pursues wicked people to make them His sons and daughters by giving up His own Son who died on the cross to pay the penalty for our wickedness so that we can receive a glorious, fulfilling life that will last forever.

Suggested Further Reading

Anderson, James N., *Why Should I Believe Christianity?* (Ross-shire: Christian Focus Publications, 2016)

Clark, Mark, *The Problem of God: Answering A Skeptics Challenges to Christianity* (Grand Rapids: Zondervan, 2017)

Coppenger, Mark, *If Christianity Is So Good, Why Are Christians So Bad?* (Ross-shire: Christian Focus Publications, 2022)

Edgar, William, *Does Christianity Really Work?* (Ross-shire: Christian Focus Publications, 2016)

Hahn, Scott and Wiker, Benjamin, *Answering the New Atheism: Dismantling Dawkins' Case Against God* (Steubenville: Emmaus Road Publishing, 2008)

Kruger, Michael J., *Surviving Religion 101: Letters to a Christian Student on Keeping the Faith in College* (Wheaton: Crossway, 2021)

McLaughlin, Rebecca, *Confronting Christianity: 12 Hard Questions for the World's Largest Religion* (Wheaton: Crossway, 2019)

Poythress, Ransom, *Richard Dawkins* (Phillipsburg: P&R Publishing, 2018)

———, *Has Science Made God Unnecessary?* (Ross-shire: Christian Focus Publications, 2022)

Robertson, David, *The Dawkins Letters: Challenging Atheist Myths*, rev. ed. (Ross-shire: Christian Focus Publications, 2007)

Smith, Christian, *Atheist Overreach: What Atheism Can't Deliver* (Oxford: Oxford University Press, 2019)

The Big Ten
Critical Questions Answered

This is a Christian apologetics series which aims to address ten commonly asked questions about God, the Bible, and Christianity. Each book, while easy to read, is challenging and thought-provoking, addressing subjects ranging from hell to science. A good read whatever your present opinions.

The books in this series are:

Why Is There Evil In The World (And So Much Of It)?
GREG WELTY

Why Should I Trust the Bible?
TIMOTHY PAUL JONES

Has Science Made God Unnecessary?
RANSOM POYTHRESS

Does Christianity Really Work?
WILLIAM EDGAR

If Christianity is So Good, why are Christians So Bad?
MARK COPPENGER

How Could a Loving God Send Anyone to Hell?
BENJAMIN M. SKAUG

Why Should I Believe Christianity?
JAMES N. ANDERSON

Why Does the God of the Old Testament
Seem so Violent and Hateful?
RICHARD P. BELCHER, JR.

Also available from Christian Focus Publications

A Christian's Pocket Guide to Loving The Old Testament
One Book, One God, One Story
Alec Motyer

- From the pen of one of the finest Old Testament scholars
- Foreword from Tim Keller
- Part of the Pocket Guide series

Many of us know and love the stories and characters of the Old Testament such as Joseph, Moses and Jonah. But how do we view its importance in relation to New Testament teaching and our 21st century experiences? This accessible yet powerful addition to the Pocket Guide series draw together the threads of Scripture to help us understand the power of God's Word when viewed in its completeness.

ISBN: 978-1-78191-580-6

ALEC MOTYER

ROOTS:
Let The Old Testament Speak

edited by John Stott

Roots:
Let the Old Testament Speak
Alec Motyer

- This is for the Christian who wants to know what the Old Testament has to do with the New Testament
- Why Christians should read the Old Testament

"The title, Old Testament, creates difficulties of its own. If it is "Old" and we are people of the "New", surely we may properly let it fade away into history? Besides, it seems very unlike the New Testament, even contradictory: all those wars when Jesus is the Prince of peace; all those commandments to obey when we are not under law but under grace. And can the God of the Old Testament be a God of love like the Father, Son and Holy Spirit?"

These are the questions that Alec Motyer, a life long lover of the Old Testament, seeks to answer starting with the conviction that Jesus is the fulfilment of the Old Testament Scripture. This is for the Christian who wants to know what the Old Testament has to do with the New Testament and why the Christian should read it.

A comprehensive survey of the Old Testament organised around its authors and major characters, the theme of this book is that the Holy Spirit chose, fashioned and equipped the biblical authors to convey distinctive truths through each of them.'

ISBN: 978-1-84550-506-6

Christian Focus Publications

Our mission statement –

STAYING FAITHFUL

In dependence upon God we seek to impact the world through literature faithful to His infallible Word, the Bible. Our aim is to ensure that the Lord Jesus Christ is presented as the only hope to obtain forgiveness of sin, live a useful life and look forward to heaven with Him.

Our books are published in four imprints:

CHRISTIAN FOCUS

Popular works including biographies, commentaries, basic doctrine and Christian living.

CHRISTIAN HERITAGE

Books representing some of the best material from the rich heritage of the church.

MENTOR

Books written at a level suitable for Bible College and seminary students, pastors, and other serious readers. The imprint includes commentaries, doctrinal studies, examination of current issues and church history.

CF4•K

Children's books for quality Bible teaching and for all age groups: Sunday school curriculum, puzzle and activity books; personal and family devotional titles, biographies and inspirational stories – because you are never too young to know Jesus!

Christian Focus Publications Ltd,
Geanies House, Fearn, Ross-shire,
IV20 1TW, Scotland, United Kingdom.
www.christianfocus.com